D1300255

MY SON'S INHERITANCE

MY SON'S INHERITANCE

A SECRET HISTORY
OF LYNCHING
AND BLOOD JUSTICE
IN INDIA

APARNA VAIDIK

ALEPH

ALEPH

ALEPH BOOK COMPANY
An independent publishing firm
promoted by *Rupa Publications India*

First published in India in 2020
by Aleph Book Company
7/16 Ansari Road, Daryaganj
New Delhi 110 002

Copyright © Aparna Vaidik 2020

All rights reserved.

The author has asserted her moral rights.

The views and opinions expressed in this book are
the author's own and the facts are as reported by her,
which have been verified to the extent possible, and
the publishers are not in any way liable for the same.

The publisher has used its best endeavours to ensure
that URLs for external websites referred to in this
book are correct and active at the time of going to
press. However, the publisher has no responsibility for
the websites and can make no guarantee that a site
will remain live or that the content is or will remain
appropriate.

No part of this publication may be reproduced,
transmitted, or stored in a retrieval system, in any
form or by any means, without permission in writing
from Aleph Book Company.

ISBN: 978-81-942337-8-7

1 3 5 7 9 10 8 6 4 2

Printed by Parksons Graphics Pvt. Ltd., Mumbai

This book is sold subject to the condition that it
shall not, by way of trade or otherwise, be lent,
resold, hired out, or otherwise circulated without the
publisher's prior consent in any form of binding or
cover other than that in which it is published.

Dedicated to
Babaji, my late grandfather,
known to everyone as Bhaiyyaji

CONTENTS

PROLOGUE

One morning, your father and I, out on our daily walk, heard sounds coming from the open area beyond the fenced boundary wall.* This open space, at the back of our colony, was once part of an old Muslim graveyard and is now an idgah, a Muslim prayer ground. The clearing was lined with trees and the graves lay towards the back. A trifle unkempt, covered with mildew, and clumps of wild grass growing around them. The open space served as a play area for the kids from Hauz Rani neighbourhood located across the road. In the evenings, elderly men, mostly Muslim shopkeepers, tailors, eatery owners, plumbers, glass workers, and car mechanics from Hauz Rani could be seen here strolling, chatting or playing cards. The open space was flanked, on one side, by a shiny new multi-speciality hospital, posh shopping malls, and a Delhi Development Authority (DDA) sports complex and on the other, the residential colony where we lived. A boundary wall cordoned off the open area from the middle-class facilities and the residential area that encircled it. Earlier, a thoroughfare cut through the open space connecting our colony with the DDA sports complex and markets on the

---

*This book is addressed to my son, whom I call babu. I hope it will help him understand his country.

other side of the graveyard. With time, the colony gate was locked and boarded up, cutting off that world from ours. I was not sure whether this had happened at the behest of the Waqf board that controlled the graveyard land or the middle-class denizens on our side of the wall.

We were walking on a narrow lane that hugged our side of the boundary wall. We had a partial view of the open space through the potted plants sitting atop the wall and the vines draping the fence. Peering through the foliage, we saw a large number of men dressed in crisp kurta-pyjamas and skullcaps sitting on the ground on sheets and mats. It was Bakra Eid and the faithful had gathered for the khutbah, the address before the namaz. We could not see the speaker, a maulana from a nearby mosque, as we were behind the stage which was covered with a small white tent. Large speakers were installed on either side of the stage and the sound of the maulana's voice, along with the sweet smell of itr, wafted across to us. The maulana urged the young men to remember that Bakra Eid symbolized qurbani, sacrifice. It was a day, he said, when they should recall the sacrifices their ancestors made towards the struggle for India's independence starting with the Battle of Plassey in 1757 and the role Siraj-ud-daulah played in it: 'Apne bade-buzurgon ki jang-i-azadi mein qurbani nahi bhulein.' Also remember the Revolt of 1857 when there was no tree where the dead bodies of Muslims were not hanging: 'Koi aisa ped nahi tha jahan mussalmano ki laashein tangi nahi thi.' India was their home: 'Ye desh aapka mulk hai.' They should not forget their history. 'Apni tareekh na bhulein' and fall for distorted versions that were being presented to them. He told them that they should also be willing to make sacrifices for their country: 'Apne mulk ke liye qurbani dene ke liye tayyar rahein.' The maulana then urged them to practise charity and to give portions of their food and money to the needy.

Your father and I walked along the boundary wall entranced by the speech and the sight of the faithful intently listening. You trailed us on your bicycle. Your father and I usually preferred a nearby park for our morning walk, not wishing to meet and chat with our kindly neighbours at this early hour, but we'd woken up late that morning and decided to do a few quick rounds inside the colony instead. Perhaps because it was late or maybe because of the loudspeakers there were fewer walkers that morning. Just then we were stopped by a friendly octogenarian who conspiratorially whispered in my ear: 'Inhone ye speakers jaan boojh kar hamari taraf lagaye hain.' These people, he said, had deliberately turned their loudspeakers towards us. The sermon was being given for our benefit. 'Ye sab hamare liye kaha ja raha hai.' He switched to English. 'Can you believe these people actually call themselves a civilization? Look at them masquerading as scholars claiming that they fought for India's independence.' A part of me wanted to walk away but your father stood there transfixed. The gentleman continued, 'I am from the Northwest Frontier Province. I know their reality better than anyone. They are all bigots and fascists.' He blamed Nehru and his government for the Partition violence and for emboldening the Muslims. 'Look around Delhi, all the Partition refugee colonies are named Rajinder

Nagar, Malviya Nagar and Patel Nagar, never Nehru Nagar. You see.' He was referring to the residential neighbourhoods of the Hindu refugees, who came to Delhi in the wake of the country's Partition in 1947, that were named after right-leaning national leaders. The neighbour claimed he had read the statement that Nathuram Godse gave during Gandhi's murder trial and he understood what must have driven that man to kill: 'Mai samajh sakta hoon ke usne kyon mara hoga.' By this time you had waited long enough and started tinkling your cycle bell, interrupting the gentleman's monologue and giving us a chance to get away. I was a tad annoyed with your father as we resumed our walk. 'Why did you keep standing there and listening? Itni der mein hamara ek round aur ho jata.' We could have walked another round in that time. He shrugged his shoulders: 'Oh! I was just being polite.' We walked home in brooding silence. I felt sad and uneasy.

The morning chores awaited us. I made my way into the kitchen and your father got busy with loading the washing machine and soaking your school shirts in the whitener. As I was preparing breakfast, a vivid memory of a silent protest I had seen on TV a few months ago came to me. It was an event that was organized to protest and grieve the spate of lynchings in the country. Some people in the crowd were holding candles, with wax slowly dripping on their fingers and singeing them lightly. Some held banners painted with bold slogans. Others stood in groups and chatted. Some were smoking. Night had fallen. It was a silent protest. The air simmered with anger, outrage, shock, and grief. I spotted several people I knew in that crowd, my associates, neighbours, and people I had met at different times in my life. There were also celebrities, social activists, and political commentators. News reporters mingled in the crowd gathering sound bites. The noise of the traffic whizzing by was audible over the microphone. A woman with pepper-grey hair, a big black bindi, and kohl-lined, eyes claimed: 'India's essence is under attack. India does not stand for violence.' A man claimed in a deep baritone: 'India is the land of Buddha and Gandhi watered by the calming waters of the Ganga. A land purified by the teachings of the Bhakti saints. The cradle of Ganga–Jamuni sanskriti.'

India, in his view, was an ocean formed by diverse human rivulets merging into it. He was claiming that the land of non-violence and tolerance was being overrun by violence and that Indian history was being bent out of shape. I remembered having the same uneasy feeling watching that programme as I did now.

As we settled down to eat our breakfast, your father brought up the morning's encounter: 'So, what do you make of Bhalla uncle's assertions?' I was still processing Bhalla uncle's monologue. Your father continued, 'I empathize with Bhalla uncle. Kya pata, unke parivar ne Partition ke dauraan bahut maar-kaat dekhi hogi.' What do we know. His family must have seen some real violence during the Partition. I said ruefully: 'Such violent experiences are like an inescapable dungeon. They trap everything inside—one's identity and perceptions.' Your father countered: 'So are you saying that their experience defies reason? They can't think outside of their experience?' I shrugged resignedly, 'Perhaps not.' He continued, 'I find Bhalla uncle's firm belief of being a victim a bit disturbing. The notion that Hindus are the only ones to have been wronged. Do you remember Manto's story "Khol do" where he describes the violence that men of the community inflicted on their women? Aur Amrita Pritam ki "Pinjar" bhi to yahi darshati hai, also depicts the same thing.'

'Hmm. You think giving people evidence to contrary or holding them to "facts" necessarily helps them question their point of view? I am not so sure telling Bhalla uncle about Manto and Amrita Pritam will make him change his narrative. You know, what I find even stranger than Bhalla uncle's claims is the one of India being a land of non-violence.' Recalling the woman at the silent protest I had seen on TV, I continued between bites of food. 'Mujhe to ahimsa ka ye dawa hi mithak lagta hai. I feel this claim of non-violence is actually a myth.' Isn't it the case that the perpetrator of violence in literature or in history is always made out to be the low-life cousin such as Duryodhana and Shishupal, or the villainous wrongdoer such as Kamsa and Ravana, or rapacious foreigners such as the Greeks, Turks, Mongols, and British? The heroes never happen to indulge in violence. They only go to war as righteous upholders of dharma or as protectors of their homeland.' I warmed up: 'Didn't they restore the moral order by killing an unarmed Karna as he changed the wheel of his chariot? Wasn't it their courage that drove them to kill their teacher, Dronacharya, by gulling him into laying down his arms by giving him the false news of his son's demise? Robbing Eklavya of his thumb so he did not contend with Arjuna for the title of the greatest archer was a righteous act, wasn't it? Defeating Duryodhana by breaking his thighs, an action forbidden in the contest, was done in the name of morality. Lakshmana was right in cutting off Surpanakha's nose for her audacious confession of love for an Aryan king. Kya fark padta hai agar saare Hindu devi-devta astra-shastra se lais hain. How does it matter if all Hindu gods come dressed with weapons of war—trident, chakra, bow and arrow, staves, spears, mace, axe—to be wielded against the unrighteous? For this reason their violence is never seen as violence in and of itself. Wo hinsa, hinsa hai hi nahi. And that's why we never stopped revering the Gita, worshipping Lord Ram or celebrating Diwali or Durga puja or the Ganapati festival.' I grew more agitated as I said, 'Kyon halla karte hain ye, so why cry foul, when some young men kill Akhlaq to avenge their dharma? Perhaps their only failing was that they killed him with their bare hands and not godly weapons.'

Just then Surinder Singhji who delivers milk every morning rang the bell. He comes all the way from the Arya Samaj gaushala in Ghazipur to deliver polybags of fresh cow milk. Your father got up to collect the milk and returned to the table after depositing them in the kitchen. I quickly finished the egg on my plate and made haste to boil the milk lest it curdled: 'Honestly, a part of me feels that believing in the idea of India being a land of non-violence abets violence by giving a free pass to all who perpetrate it. In some ways, it makes us accomplices in a conspiracy of wilful ignorance even as we speak up for humanity and as we decry the death penalty. I sometimes wonder if it is conscious forgetfulness or honest naiveté on our part.'

◆

You know, babu, they say Zahid Ahmad, Noman, Mohammed Akhlaq, Mazloom Ansari, Imtiaz Khan, Mustain Abbas, Vashram Sarvaiya and his brothers, Mokati Elisa and Pehlu Khan, were all killed 'at the hands of persons unknown'. By a mob, bheed ne mara. A mass of people indistinguishable from each other in their desire for collective retribution. Since everyone is guilty, in effect, no one is guilty. The distribution of guilt amongst the crowd dilutes it. Neuters it. Disembodies it. But here is the secret. They were actually killed at the hands of persons known. We know their names. We know their faces. We grew up with them. Celebrated their joyous birth. Took morning walks with them. Shared meals with them. Attended their weddings. Hosted them in our home. We see them each morning staring back at us as we brush our teeth. They are us. Wo hum hain. The people on our side of the boundary wall.

The ones who invoked non-violence as India's essence are not much different from the ones who empathized with Godse. Let me take a slight detour and say that quite often the invocation of India's composite tradition and the Bhakti movement conveniently helps us set aside conversation about caste oppression. As if the world of syncretic culture and the egalitarian ideology of the Bhakti saints inoculates us against casteism. It helps us 'de-caste' ourselves while keeping our caste privilege intact. In a similar fashion, we presume that our self is unsullied by violence. You may not know this, or maybe you do, the essence of Indian civilization is also violence. Hinsa bhi tumhari dharohar hai. Violence is also India's heritage that has been bequeathed from generation to generation. The history of tolerance is also one of tolerance towards violence.

Should we be mourning the killing of 'beef criminals'? Or is it the perversion of the souls of the 'witnesses' of lynching that should be lamented? Or again is it our family, friends, and fellow Indians who treat these killings as retribution— payback time for these communities that one ought to mourn? Or the people who capitalize on these killings to strengthen and bind the majoritarian community across class, caste, generational, and regional divides? Or those who righteously ask why a death of a Hindu does not create such a furore? The perpetrators of this violence have not always been the state, the rulers, the police or the army but also our silence. Our looking away from inconvenient truths, our blindness to our social privilege, and in our ability to pass off our unearned privilege as merit or as advantages earned by hard work. It makes us either remain silent or glorify non-violence as our essence. This is how, babu, we let our silence lynch our souls.

1

THE STORY OF BHARMALL

The last student entered my office and settled on the chair next to me. I had arranged my room so the table was set against the wall and didn't stand between me and anyone who came to visit. I could sense some tension beneath the calm of his face. The young man kept flipping the pages of the book he was holding. He looked me in the eye and asked: 'Professor, why should I study history? What purpose does it serve?' He asked gently but it was clear that he had been struggling with this question for a while and had somehow gathered the courage to come to my office seeking an answer. I wondered if this was a simple query about studying history or whether it was an existential question. Why do I exist and what does knowing about the human past do for my existence? I wasn't quite prepared to field the unexpected philosophical question about history at that hour of the day. But I also knew that I could not send him away without an answer. I sat back in my chair feeling rather inadequate. I gave him a tentative answer: 'Studying history for me is like darshan, celestial viewing.'

I knew right away that wasn't the best answer because he shot back a quizzical glance. I had to now explain darshan to him. Suddenly I remembered Ramdhari Singh Dinkar's epic poem *Rashmirathi* and my initial hesitation dissipated and words flowed. In *Rashmirathi,* the poet depicts a scene of the Kaurava prince Duryodhana's royal court. Lord Krishna had gone there as a messenger of peace beseeching Duryodhana not to go to war. Duryodhana, instead of offering a seat to Krishna, ordered the royal guards to arrest him. Krishna challenged Duryodhana to chain him. In this moment, Krishna, a celestial being, increased the scale of his human form, 'Apna swaroop vistaar kiya', and his body became a resplendent tableau. This was the viraat roop, supreme form. The overawed courtiers beheld the dazzling vision. They saw how the eternal stream of life and death flowed from It; that the sounds of the entire universe were embodied in It; that immortality and annihilation, all resided in It. 'Sab janm mujhi se paate hain, phir laut mujhi mein aate hain.' The viraat roop was a storehouse of human memories, its pasts, where one could trace the ebb and flow of human existence, the battles and the friendships, and the sounds and visions of the universe. Much like Alice's Looking Glass or Dumbledore's Pensieve, the viraat roop unlocked mysteries, divulged secrets, whispered the silences and harboured clues to human existence.

'Witnessing the viraat roop was darshan,' I concluded, 'History is darshan.' The student sat there listening to me. In trying to answer his question, I had ended up giving him access to my mind. I felt a bit exposed and vulnerable. All theories of history were after all supposed to flow from the West and here I was reciting not even Bengali but Hindi poetry to him. He looked at me trying to absorb what I had just said. We sat in silence for a while. A faint smile grew on his face as he said, 'That makes sense.' I was relieved as he left my office holding on to a thought that had just illuminated a small corner of his being; at least I hoped it had.

As I sat there looking out of the window, the memory of my grandfather came to me unbidden. He was the reason I became a historian. I remembered him with fondness and pain. He was short-statured and stocky. He had sparse, straight white hair and a wide forehead. His large, piercing eyes crinkled up at the corners when he smiled. The petite handlebar moustache of his younger days grew into a wide one that merged into a long, flowing beard in his old age. The white unkempt beard made his eyes look even sharper. He laughed heartily and had immense capacity for dialogue. He could converse for hours. He also possessed considerable physical strength. I remember him carrying bags of iron goods, that were almost impossible to move, which he would purchase from Old Delhi to take back to Indore, where he lived and ran a hardware shop. He and I would have long debates that would slowly turn into arguments about everything under the sun. I often had no good arguments to rebut his. He had gradually started plying me with books by an Indore-born Maharashtrian author, P. N. Oak. These books were exposés of historical conspiracies around Mughal monuments in India. Each book focused on a particular monument—a fort, a palace or a mosque, and attempted to show how it was, in reality, a Hindu structure that had been desecrated and appropriated by Muslim rulers. I had read these books with neither belief nor disbelief. At the time, I didn't know what to make of them. But nevertheless, they stayed with me and made me want to know more. I was curious. Through these books, I acquired an abiding interest in Delhi's architectural heritage and eventually went on to study history in college.

In between all the arguments and conversations, there was one oft-repeated story, a garbled and half-baked tale of a brave ancestor from Rajasthan, that remained stuck in my memory through my childhood and into the adult years. The name of this ancestor appears in the family bahi, an account ledger, as Bharmall. My grandfather was born into a Marwari family of Vaishnav Baniyas that is known to safeguard and cherish their bahis. Bharmall had entered the hoary precincts of history for having immolated himself over a social cause. There came a time where I wanted to know more about this ancestor. I had just returned from England after finishing my higher studies. The best starting point would have been my grandfather but our relationship had been strained for a while. He had opposed my going to England. He had sent my parents a ten-page fax with his views on why that education would corrupt me. But I set aside my rancour and approached him for the details of Bharmall's story. To my surprise, he proposed that we make a trip to his ancestral town of Khatu in Rajasthan. It was also known as Khatu Shyamji and was a famous pilgrimage centre.

◆

My grandfather and I reached Khatu Shyamji on the sudi gyaras, the eleventh day of the 'bright fortnight'. The sleepy mofussil town of Khatu Shyamji seemed to have awakened to a riot of colours and sounds as thousands of pilgrims came pouring into the town to worship at the Shyamji Temple devoted to Lord Krishna. The pilgrims marched into the town carrying festoons and banners, jostling with each other for God's favour. Some arrived in motor vehicles and many on foot. The ardour of devotees crawling on all fours on hot sand to the temple and touching their foreheads to the ground created a spectacle that inspired faith and astonishment. My grandfather and I were also pilgrims of a different kind. As we walked along, I could not help wonder what drew people in such multitudes to the town.

After briefly visiting Shyamji Temple, we made our way to Bharmall's shrine known as Bharmall ka sata. The caretaker of the shrine informed us that about seventy-five years ago some people, by chance, unearthed a stone tablet while digging up the place to build a house. The stone tablet narrated Bharmall's story. An influential zamindar, he is said to have served as an official at the court of the local raja. They say that one day a local Muslim butcher was forcibly walking away with some cows that he intended to slaughter. Bharmall swore that if the butcher were to take away the cows he would immolate himself in protest. The butcher paid no heed to Bharmall's anxious declarations and mercilessly dragged the cows away. Bharmall, a brave warrior, true to his honour, immolated himself. A stone tablet, which narrated this heroic story of the courageous warrior, was erected at the place where Bharmall self-immolated and the tablet's discovery led to a shrine being built on that spot.

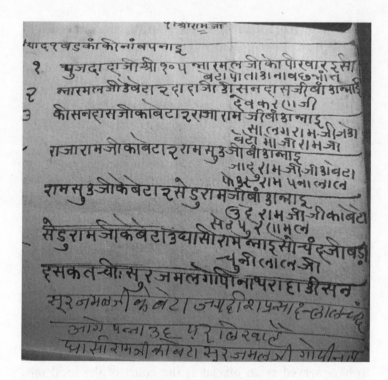

Family bahi with Bharmall's name

A 'sata', as my grandfather told me, was the masculine form of the word sati. Sati was the ancient practice of wives immolating themselves on the funeral pyres of their dead husbands. Rajasthan is dotted with numerous sati shrines. Supernatural and healing powers have come to be associated with Bharmall's shrine. It has become a tradition in the area for newly-weds, besides others, to visit the shrine for blessings for a blissful conjugal life and a well-endowed household. It is

6

said that an offering of a brinjal and a broom cures moles on one's body. Bharmall's shrine, perhaps, derived its religious significance from being situated in the vicinity of the great Shyamji Temple.

The sun had begun to make its journey towards the horizon by the time we were done exploring the town. My grandfather and I gathered our stuff for the return trip. As we trudged back to our van, despite the festive atmosphere of the town, our mood was sombre. It had been a long day. As the van sped through the dusty streets, it shook and vibrated like a man racked by a bronchial cough. My grandfather clasped my hand to steady himself. As I held his frail hand in mine, a whole new meaning of the word 'history' unfolded before me. A history without chronology, without a beginning and an end, and one without kings and queens. This history was about us, how it separated yet conjoined our lives.

◆

I travelled to Khatu Shyamji over two decades ago with my grandfather to see the shrine. I wish I had asked him what Bharmall's story meant to him. He is no longer there to answer this question but, as a historian, I continue to wonder. How am I to understand this story? Is this yet another tale that captures the cruelty and insensitivity of the beef-eating Muslim and the Hindu hero who rescues the gaumata? Or is there another reading of this story? I began researching the history of Rajasthan, reading books, and talking to scholars in order to make sense of the complex filaments of regional history. I soon realized that the story had its fount in seventeenth-century Rajasthan when Vaishnavism and the Rajput community together came to dominate its history. This was the time when the map of Rajasthan looked nothing like it does in geography books today. It did not have the present-day boundaries. Its borders were like those of an amoeba, changing form with various empires, kingdoms, communities, social groups, languages, and cultures holding sway at various times.

Our story begins in the seventeenth-century when a Vaishnavite sect known as the Pushti Marg acquired predominance in Rajasthan. This was the time when the Mughal emperors held sway over northern India and had made alliances with local rulers in Rajputana and other parts of India to give stability to their empire. The Pushti Marg was founded by a fifteenth-century saint, Vallabhacharya (1479–1531). He lived in the region of Braj, that is, the areas around the cities of Mathura and Vrindavan that were traditonally associated with mythological stories of Krishna's life. For Vallabhacharya, Krishna was the supreme lord from whom all creation emanated. Human liberation was to come through the cultivation of passionate devotion to Krishna. In this, Vallabhacharya was in line with the Bhakti tradition of previous centuries that thrived on devotional worship of the supreme being. The difference was that, unlike the other contemporary Bhakti saints such as Kabir, Dadu Dayal, and Ravidas, who came from the lower castes, denounced the caste system, mocked ritualism and believed in nirguna bhakti or worshipping the formless supreme being, Vallabhacharya was a Brahmin who believed in the maintenance of the socio-ritual order, the varnashrama dharma, and believed in saguna worship (God with a form). Vallabhacharya's sect was similar to that of Chaitanya Mahaprabhu (1486–1533), another Vaishnavite saint from Bengal. Chaitanya Mahaprabhu's devotees, known as the Gaudiyas, had migrated from Bengal to Braj to spread his message. Both the Pushti Margis and the Gaudiyas congregated in Braj and made it a hub of Vaishnavite pilgrimage. Their followers primarily belonged to the mercantile Baniya community of Gujarat.

Over the next century, in order to ensure stability and sustenance, the Vaishnavite gurus known as maharajas, sought political patronage of the Mughal nobility who granted them tax-free land in return for religious blessings. The Gaudiyas, for instance, were patronized by Raja Todar Mal and Raja Man Singh who were Hindu nobles at the court of Mughal emperor Akbar. Donation from wealthy Baniya devotees belonging to big mercantile centres such as Surat, Ahmedabad, and Bombay further enhanced the power and prestige of the maharajas. With time, the relationship between the maharajas, their political patrons, and the Baniya community deepened. Hereafter, Vaishnavism would flourish in Braj and Gujarat supported by the sinews of merchant capital and imperial power.

It was in the seventeenth century that the Vaishnava maharajas turned their attention towards Rajasthan. The Jat rebellions against the Mughal empire created political instability in Braj prompting the Pushti Marg gurus to seek refuge in territories controlled by Rajput clans. The Vaishnava maharajas as they settled in Rajasthan brought with them

Braj culture and its language, the Brajbhasha. As a literary variant of Hindi, Brajbhasha encompassed several different poetic worlds from folk to courtly to the religious. By the late sixteenth century, many poets at the Mughal courts and later at the Rajput durbars were specialists in Brajbhasha and so were the families of musicians and dancers who performed at the temples and the royal durbars in Rajasthan. Abdul Rahim Khan-i-Khana, Keshavdas, Amrita Rai, Narottama Dasa, Padmakar, Dungarsi Ratanu, Durasa Adha were some of the court poets and charan, the folk poets of Braj. The songs of the Rajasthani Manganiyar performers preserve to this day the linguistic form of Brajbhasha that has died out in the region of Braj.

Brajbhasha kavya, literary narratives, were an important catalyst in ensuring political patronage for the Vaishnava gurus. At the heart of the world of Brajbhasha kavya was the figure of Lord Krishna as the supreme being but also as the model Hindu king. For the Rajput rulers the allure of Vaishnavism lay in this image of Krishna. The rulers' depiction as the incarnation or the embodiment of Krishna by their court poets legitimized their authority and positioned them as upholders and defenders of the Hindu dharma. The Braj poets at the Rajput courts also created imaginary vanshavali, genealogies for the Rajput kings tracing their lineage back to the Suryavansha, the solar dynasty of Lord Ram or the Chandravansha, the lunar dynasty from which the Pandavas and Krishna were believed to have descended. The Brajbhasha kavya while furnishing the Rajput rulers with royal lineages also seamlessly lauded the Mughal emperors so as to ensure that the Rajput rulers' increasing power and prestige did not incur the Mughal emperor's wrath, especially in cases where the Rajputs were serving as nobles at the Mughal court.

The Rajput rulers who embraced Vaishnavism consequently undertook intense temple-building activity and the consecration of older temples in turn reinvigorated pilgrim activity. The Rajput royal ceremonies also began to closely imitate the temple rituals. This was in keeping with the new raj dharma or the normative ideal of kingship which had religious patronage at its core. Patronizing religious groups and their temples, in turn, also allowed the Rajput rulers to assert their traditional duties as patrons of religion and art. Temple-building and religious patronage enhanced their political prestige and influence in the region, especially in relation to the rival kingdoms. The rulers of Mewar, for instance, were able to regain their lost political glory by becoming energetic Vaishnava patrons. The Mewar dynasty's political patronage enabled the Vaishnava gurus to acquire visibility and influence that, in turn, begot them even more patrons such as the royal courts of Bikaner, Jaipur, Kota, and Kishangarh. In time, the maharajas reacquired their glory and transformed into wealthy landowners as they were in Braj. Their position became so strong that in the years to come they would continue to enjoy pre-eminence even when the political fortunes of some of the royal patrons declined.

Vaishnavism's growth in Rajasthan was thus intertwined with the political ascendancy of the Rajputs; many of them went from being sedentary agricultural communities to becoming the ruling clans of Rajasthan. For the subject population who primarily comprised cattle-herding, pastoral, tribal, and mercantile communities, the image of Krishna (as a gwala, cowherd, who is a keeper and protector of cattle) had deep emotional and moral resonance. Cattle (cows, oxen, and bulls) were an important form of wealth in the region's economy which was shaped by its semi-arid climate. In the local language the words used for cattle and wealth were same: dhan, maal, and vitt. Even some of the pastoral communities such as Dhangars and Maldharis derived their names from these words. Protecting cattle from disease, death, and raids was woven into the social fabric of the cattle-owning pastoral communities and it distinguished their culture from that of the trading communities. Thus the Rajput ruler's association with the image of Krishna as the protector of cattle and as an arbitrator of disputes involving cattle along with religious patronage of the Vaishnava gurus went a long way towards sanctifying his claim to the throne.

One sees a concurrent growth in the Rajputization of local deities or 'saint-warriors', known as jujhars, who were worshipped as livestock saviours (protectors of cattle and camels). Jujhar is derived from the word jujharu which means combative, relentless, implacable, and courageous. These elements are borne out by mythic stories of a jujhar warrior's torso relentlessly fighting with swords in both hands even after being decapitated by cow robbers. The jujhar returns home victorious with the cows, eyes having appeared on his chest and a lotus flower in place of his head. A shrine is built where his body had fallen off the horse. Traditionally, appeasement and worship of deities who protected cattle and horses from epidemics, maladies, snake or scorpion bites, and cattle-raiders were integral aspects of the lives of the pastoral communities. The entire region of Khatu Shyamji is littered with a number of hero-stones commemorating jujhars who died protecting cattle. Many of the jujhar deities were Rajputs such as Baba Ramdevji, Gogapir, Harbhuji, Pabuji, Tallinathji or Jat deities such as Biggaji and Tejaji who were preservers of the nomadic lifestyle.

As is common with local shrines, some of these deities, also known as pirs, were worshipped by Hindus and Muslims alike. For instance, Gogapir (a serpent God and gau bhagat, a protector of cows) is worshipped as Gogaveer or Jujharveer by Hindus and as Guga or Zahirpir by Muslims. However, both Hindus and Muslims who worship Gogapir primarily come from lower castes and peasant-pastoral communities such as Chamars, Mirasans, Kalbelias, and Gaduliyas. Goga was a pir who was worshipped not only in the area we know today as Rajasthan but also in Punjab and present-day Haryana and by the Jat, Gujar, and Sikh communities in the region. Although the cult of Goga can be traced back to the eleventh century, from the seventeenth century onwards the historical texts start mentioning him as a Chauhan Rajput and by the nineteenth century he acquires a firm Rajput identity. Rajputization thus closely associated the Jujhar deities with the Vaishnava version of cow protection. Perhaps Bharmall was one such Vaishnava jujhar.

Incidentally, the story of Bharmall is also quite similar to an unusual story of Goma sati. In her story, a roaming band of cow robbers steal cows from Goma's village. On the way they meet Goma who is a low-caste Charan woman. She halts them and demands to know where they are taking the cows. The robbers confess that they have stolen the cows but refuse to give them up. She blocks their way and threatens to cut off her limbs if they take away the cows. The robbers disregard her warnings and Goma kills herself. The name Goma probably means go-ma, that is cow-mother or mother cow. She is worshipped in different parts of Rajasthan by Hindus and Muslims alike.

With the growing predominance of Vaishnavism there was a symbolic shift in the way cattle and cattle-protection were perceived. Cattle that were until now simply a valuable economic resource gradually began to be seen as sacred, and cattle-protection was transformed into a sacred duty. Instead of the cattle-saviour being the deity, it was the cattle that became the object of worship. The symbolism associated with cattle had separated the pre-Vaishnavite socio-cultural world of Rajasthan from that of Braj. In Rajasthan, cattle were integral to the existence of pastoral communities, an economic resource that was coveted, fought over, and protected but one that was not sacred in the way it was in the religio-cultural cosmos of Braj. The shift towards sacralization of the cow had significant implications for the local economy. It began to rupture the traditional network of Rajasthan's agro-pastoral economy where cattle rearing was part of an intricate network of economic exchange that involved not just the cattle-breeders but equally the traders, skinners, tanners, butchers, and leatherworkers. The prosperous leather goods industry in the region thrived on this network. However, all the auxiliary economic activities associated with cattle-rearing such as raiding, slaughtering, skinning, tanning, and the consumption of cattle began to be frowned upon as the cow became sacred. Gauraksha, the protection of cattle, serendipitously shifted in meaning from protecting the cow from diseases, snakebites, epidemics, and raiders to protecting it from the butcher, specifically the 'Muslim' butcher as the one in Bharmall's tale.

Does this explain why the abductor of cattle in Bharmall's tale was a 'Muslim' butcher and not just another Rajput cattle raider? Yes, possibly. There is a possibility that the Muslim butcher in the tale belonged to the aforementioned Dhangar community that specialized in cattle breeding. The subgroups within the Dhangar community keep goats and sheep or weave blankets. Today, the Dhangars are spread out in the region of Rajasthan, Maharashtra, Karnataka, and Andhra Pradesh. Presumably one of the multiple endogamous subgroups of the Dhangar community converted to Islam in the thirteenth century. They started slaughtering animals as a response to the growing meat market. Since the market demand was driven by Muslim consumers these Dhangars converted to Islam in order to fulfil the canonical requirements for halal meat. Although the Dhangar subgroup converted to Islam, they retained their rural and pastoral caste identity. Between the eighth to thirteenth centuries, several communities in the Indian subcontinent had converted to Islam. The reasons for conversions ranged from the influence of Sufi saints, opportunities for economic and political advancement,

The arid landscape of Rajasthan with babool trees; the Aravalli mountains can be seen in the background.

Rajasthan landscape

proximity to Muslim rulers, social liberation and armed coercion. According to historian Richard Eaton, the most extensive conversion took place not amongst the literate settled agricultural communities but amongst non-literate pastoral and forest communities inhabiting the fringes of Hindu agrarian society and the frontiers of the Muslim state (as in East Bengal and West Punjab). As in the case of the Jats, conversion to Islam facilitated a sedentary life and transformation from pastoralism into agriculturalists. The affiliation to Islam came with minimal changes in pre-conversion religious practices and many groups retained their original cosmological universe and continued to maintain their social or caste location. That is, people continued to believe in Allah (refraining from eating pork, practising circumcision, and burying the dead) but at the same time continued to participate in Janmashtami and Durga Puja celebrations or worship deities to ward off diseases or use Hindu astrologers and almanacs. With the caste order intact, the social group for centuries continued to function and live as they did previously despite the gradual change in their religious identity. There are several instances of individuals with dual religious identities such as Nizari Hasan Kabiruddin in the fifteenth century who was known as a Suhrawardi Sufi Pir, Hasad Darya, and a Shaiva ascetic, Anand-jo-Dhani. Another famous figure is Himmat Bahadur, a Muslim warlord who was also a Gosain warrior, Anup Giri. The Meos of Mewat, the Langa and Manganiyar communities of folk musicians from Rajasthan, the Kyamkhanis in northern Rajasthan were also social groups that converted to Islam but continued to

17

be identifed as Rajputs, an affiliation 'considered exclusively Hindu in India today'. Similar was the case of the Muslim Dhangars. Although unsubstantiated by definitive historical evidence, there is a possibility that once Vaishnavism took root, Khatik, the Hindu butcher community, distanced itself from handling cows and the Muslim butcher who had been slaughtering cattle for the meat market for centuries continued his trade. It seems with the growing sacralization of cows, the traditional trade of the Muslim butcher began to offend Hindu religious sensibilities and it is in this form the Muslim butcher entered Bharmall's story.

2

MY GRANDFATHER—THE ARYAN

As I pored over books on the history of Rajasthan to reconstruct the historical context for Bharmall's story, I began to ask why this story held such deep meaning for my grandfather. Surely he was unaware of the history of Vaishnavism in Rajasthan as a lot of this research was recent. So was Bharmall's story more than an ancestor's tale for my grandfather? Why was it told and retold? It probably gave him emotional succour and a sense of rootedness. He was born in 1924. His mother died when he was still an infant and he lost his father when he was three. Brought up first by his nani and maasi and later by his chachi and cousin he always had a roof over his head and enough to eat but remained emotionally derelict. In 1940, at the age of sixteen, he started out as a letter-writer for immigrant labourers in the local post office. To earn more money, he would send telegrams, money orders, and parcels for them. Gradually he began to bring in a regular income that was more than that of the postmaster. He felt, for an orphan, it was his good fortune to have become eligible for marriage. He married my grandmother in 1943. He soon set up a hardware shop in the bustling Loha Mandi in Siyaganj, Indore, where he sold iron weights, weighing scales, treasure chests, and chains. He sired six children, the eldest of whom was my father who came to Delhi for higher studies and made the city his home. His need for connecting back to a family heritage seemed to be a plausible answer but not a sufficient one. Knowing him I felt there had to be more to these retellings. I wondered whether my grandfather's fascination with Bharmall's story had to do with the times he grew up in?

These questions led me into the world of nineteenth-century India, the age of the British Raj. Researching this trail was like falling through a rabbit hole and arriving in the city of Babel, a vast and fascinating world of numerous languages. The European colonization of India had occasioned a novel encounter between the languages of the Indian subcontinent with the ones of Europe. A great number of European scholars, known as philologists, began to engage in the comparative study of these languages. Philological research went beyond an analysis of construction of words and rules of grammar. It included the study of formation of languages, their origins and their history and the examination of literal texts as oral records. The philologists believed that languages gave direct access to the human mind and had the potential to unlock the secrets of human origins. One of the most astounding claims the philologists put forward in 1786 was that the Sanskrit language possessed European roots. They established that the languages of India (Sanskrit), Iran (old Persian), and Europe (Latin, Greek, Gothic, Celtic) had a common genealogy and were separate from Arabic and Turkish languages. Sanskrit's racio-linguistic affinity with the European languages was a revolutionary idea as it suggested historical linkages between the spatially-disparate territories of Europe, Iran, and India. The academic discipline of comparative philology drew strength from and thrived on revealing such historical connections that were otherwise lost in historical and collective memory. Energized by the discovery of these new connections, in 1816, it was discovered that the Indo-European group of languages were separate not just from Arabic and Turkish but also the Dravidian languages (Tamil, Telugu, and Kannada) of southern India. At this time the idea that languages embodied or were markers of the racial identity of human groups was a very strong one. As a result the philological differences were not simply about groups of people speaking different languages but seen as markers of 'racial' difference. That is, it was the language one spoke rather than one's complexion that was the true marker of one's race. This made fair-skinned Sanskrit and dark-skinned Dravidian speakers two different and antagonistic racial groups. The clash between the two was believed to have given rise to the Indian caste system.

This discovery had important implications for the history of the Indian subcontinent. It spawned a new theory regarding the peopling of India. The philologists identified the Sanskrit-speaking Aryans as the distant cousins of the white Europeans who immigrated to India around 1500 BCE. Some scholars, however, believed that India was the original home of the Aryans. Irrespective of whether the Aryans were immigrants or aboriginal, the new research in languages established that Indians were the Aryans, composers of the Vedas and builders of ancient Indian civilization. At the time, the announcement of the 'discovery' of the Indus Valley Civilization as the most ancient civilization of the subcontinent (in 1924) was several decades away. Once the civilization was discovered, it disturbed the neat theorization regarding the Aryans as builders of Indian civilization. It gave rise to two antagonistic views: first, the ones who believed Aryans were immigrants presumed that the Indus civilization preceded the Aryan/Vedic civilization and was destroyed by the latter; second, the ones who believed the Aryans to be indigenous reckoned that the Indus civilization was the Vedic civilization. Either way the belief that the Aryans were builders of Indian civilization remained unshaken. It had become the master narrative of Indian history.

This racio-linguistic theory of the peopling of India and the making of its civilization gradually seeped into all academic writing generating a sophisticated body of knowledge embodied in various academic disciplines such as philology, archaeology, history, and anthropology. The Orientalist scholars not only upheld the Aryans as the builders of Indian civilization but also believed that India represented the innocent childhood, the lost soul of Europe, and an escape from the industrial West. They saw India as having cultural traits that were the converse of the 'West' whose essence was rationality, scientific thought, and the institutions of liberal capitalism and democracy. Indian thought in comparison was mythic and symbolic instead of being rational and logical. India's essence, in their view, was in collectivism reflected in its caste system than in Western-style individualism. Thus started the glorification of India as a land of spirituality. The writings of Orientalists also implicitly justified British rule in India. As a part of the romanticization of India, the idea of the Noble Savage began to take shape—a creature who is noble because of its innocence but an uncivilized being nevertheless; and thus not possessing the capacity for self-rule. The Orientalists thus saw British rule as a period of tutelage until the present-day Indians came of age.

Orientalist imagery permeated the writings of Indian reformers in the nineteenth century who were struggling with the question of India's subordination. The idea that Indians were Aryans had caught their imagination. The valorization of India, its ancient past, the age of the Aryans and their civilization acquired new wheels. Starting from Raja Ram Mohan Roy to Keshub Chandra Sen, Swami Dayanand Saraswati, Mahadev Govind Ranade, Bal Gangadhar Tilak, and Vivekananda to Gandhi, all subscribed to the idea that the Aryans were the builders of Indian civilization and the composers of the Vedas. The Vedic texts came to be seen as embodying the earliest and, therefore, the purest form of religion. Tradition as it resided in the Vedic corpus was deemed timeless, transhistorical, and unsullied. It was sanatan, i.e., eternal. This sanatan dharma, however, had been degraded with the passage of time as a result of contact with barbarian Others—the dark-skinned Dravidians, the forest-dwelling Adivasis, the invading Muslims, and the Christians. This sanatan tradition, therefore, was in need of 'reform'. The social reformers focused their critique not on the pure Vedic 'texts' but the everyday corrupt 'practice' of religion. They believed that the undefiled Vedic religion was retrievable through the application of rationality. This was a new Judaeo-Christian understanding of 'religion' that measured one's relationship with the divine on terms set by rationality.

All the nineteenth-century Indian reformers in their quest for the pure Vedic religion unequivocally saw the post-Vedantic religion as being ridden with ritualism and superstition and blamed the Brahmins for concealing the Vedantic knowledge. They rejected polytheism, condemned idol worship, and focused on 'spirituality', that is, a religiosity independent of ritual. In their view, the need was to first retrieve the golden age (i.e. the Vedic age); second, purge it of the false accretions that had occurred with the passage of time; and, third, to disseminate it to the masses in the vernacular. The abolition of sati, the passing of the Child Marriage Act and the Age of Consent Act followed from this premise. In their understanding, the glorious Aryan tradition was synonymous with 'Hindu'. From this evolved the notion of Hindu universalism, the idea of Hinduism as a civilization coterminous with the idea of India—spiritual and non-violent—a utopia of the Aryans. In upholding the myth of Aryan superiority, the reformers posited the Hindu civilization as one that was interrupted by and corrupted during the 'Muslim rule'. The Hindu and the Islamic thus came to be seen as two mutually exclusive and autonomous heritages.

The Aryan utopia was the point of departure for the writings of Indian reformers. Swami Vivekananda

(1863–1902), for instance, believed that the superiority of the Aryan civilization came from its inclusiveness. In his view, the Aryans did not settle in India by annihilating the first inhabitants, rather, they absorbed them. The Aryans were inclusive despite their cultural superiority. The Aryan civilization's strength thus lay in its 'central assimilative core', in its tolerance (i.e., non-violence) and in its accommodation of diversity. Vivekananda further made use of this argument to account for the origin of the caste system. According to him, caste as a device of social organization brought together different racial groups under the civilizing influence of the Aryans. He took the ecumenical and benign view of the caste system as simply a way of organizing society's labour. For him, the caste system was 'originally' occupational and unrelated to one's birth. In his view, the argument that it was related to birth was a corruption that had occurred along the way. It was the Aryan civilization's tolerance, spirituality, and philosophy of non-violence that had made it resilient despite several ferocious attacks from foreigners. The Turkish invasions, raiding of Somnath, misrule by the Mughal kings, the British blowing Kuka rebels from the mouth of cannons and the brutal repression of the Revolt of 1857 were some of the glaring instances of foreign brutality. Violence was something, therefore, that the Muslims and the British did. Aryan civilization was non-violent.

The writings of Swami Dayanand Saraswati (1824–83), a Gujarati Brahmin, and the founder of Arya Samaj, a reformist organization (established in 1875) took these arguments further. He performed an incredibly imaginative feat by placing not simply spirituality, tolerance, and non-violence at the core of the Aryan identity but also cow protection. Dayanand Saraswati wrote *Satyarth Prakash* (The Light of Truth) in 1875 and a tract entitled *Gaukarunanidhi* (Treasure of Mercy for Cow) in 1881 in which he established that the 'Arya' identity was coterminus with Hindu identity and premised on the non-consumption of beef. Beef-eating, according to the *Satyarth Prakash* was a dietary practice of 'carnivorous and intemperate foreigners', that is, the Christians and Mahomedans. He wrote: 'These foreigners took to drinking wine and eating beef and other kinds of flesh.' Even their Gods were meat-eaters unlike those of Aryavarta, the land of the Hindus. Citing the rules of Vedic grammar and vocabulary he also refuted the general impression that the Ashwamedha (horse sacrifice) and Gomedh (cow-killing) prescribed in Vedas referred to the killing of horses and cows in ceremonies. The Aryans held cattle to be sacred and therefore could never have killed it.

In *Gaukarunanidhi*, Dayanand made persuasive arguments regarding the cow's sacredness based on its value as a milch and a farm animal. He believed that a cow's milk in comparison to a buffalo's was aarogyakarak aur buddhivardhak, that is, it had greater ability to provide a healthy constitution and intellectual rigour. The milk of one cow and its six female progeny over the course of their lives was calculated to feed nearly a hundred and fifty thousand persons. In comparison, their meat would satisfy only eighty people at a time. He further argued that the slaughter of cows increased the cost of cattle, milk, milk products, and also contributed to the decline of agriculture, which in turn pushed up foodgrain prices. Having established the cow's economic utility and the superiority of its milk, Dayanand's text slips into a dialogue between 'hinsak', the one who does violence, and 'rakshak', the one who protects. The hinsak begins by asking why meat-eating was considered wrong if it was not prohibited by one's religion. The rakshak responds by redefining religion or dharma as righteous conduct that did not violate anyone. To kill animals was an irreligious and sinful act. In response to another of the hinsak's questions, the rakshak replies: 'Jin ke doodh aadi khane peene mein aate hain, ve mata-pita ke samaan mananeeya kyon na hone chahiye?' From whom one derives milk for consumption, shouldn't they be honoured like one's parents? This rhetorical question elevated the cow to the status of the mother and firmly established the need to care for it as one would a parent.

The text then goes on to prescribe the rules for becoming a gaurakshak and the duties of one; along with the structure, rules, regulations, and the roles of the office bearers of a gaurakshini sabha, the cow protection society. The basic rules that a person had to observe in order to serve as a gaurakshak were: acquiring knowledge of Vedic literature, maintaining cordiality, generosity, and collegiality with other sabha members, resolving interpersonal differences amicably, committing to provide for orphans and widows, raising funds to arrange for the upkeep of young and old cows, drawing milk from the cow only when the calf was satisfied and had grown to a certain stage, transferring the animals in one's care to others in the sabha if one were unable to take care of them and so on. *Gaukarunanidhi* promised the gaurakshaks that they were sure to reap the rewards of their righteous deeds in this world and beyond. Couched in the language of economic rationality and righteous conduct, the idea of cow protection appeared in keeping with the modernity of the times and was presented as a secular duty of all 'Aryavarti deshvasi', all the countrymen residing in Aryavarta, the ancient land of the Aryans. Hereafter, the Arya Samaj became the main organization spearheading the campaign to protect the cow.

My grandfather embraced the Arya Samaj sometime after his marriage in the 1940s. In one of the pamphlets that he wrote after taking sannyas (i.e., becoming vanprasthi and retiring from his duties as a householder), he talks about his gradual conversion from being a Shiva bhakt to becoming a devout Arya Samaji. He was a regular visitor to the Shiva temple in Indore's cchavni (cantonment) area. Once during a night-long rudrabhishek (special worship ceremony associated with Lord Shiva), he and his friends lulled by the rhythmic recitation of the mantras began to nod off. In order to stay awake, he asked the pandit to pause and explain the meaning of the mantras as he recited them. The pandit's response surprised my grandfather when the former nonchalantly said that he did not know the meaning of any of the mantras of the rudrabhishek. This incident stayed with my grandfather. A year later, he found a thick, dog-eared book with the front and last pages torn out that had all the mantras along with their meanings. He began to devour the book as it revealed the meaning of the mantras and gave him a lot of other information. However, he did not know the name of the book. He was told later by a friend that the book's name was *Satyarth Prakash* and that he could visit an Arya Samaj mandir on Sunday and get a new copy. Thereafter, he began to visit the Arya Samaj mandir every Sunday. Initially, he feared the consequences of not worshipping the idol of Shiva but gradually he stopped going to the Shiva temple. He voraciously read all the writings of Swami Dayanand. Dayanand was flowing against the grain of everything he knew about Hinduism. He found Dayanand's irreverence astounding and fascinating. He began to encourage his wife to accompany him to the Arya Samaj mandir. She began to read the writings of Swami Dayanand and slowly stopped performing the Brahmanical rituals. He was grateful to have her complete cooperation in the matter. As the kids were born, Arya Samaji values were instilled in them.

If there was a spindle around which his life-thread was wound, it was the Arya Samaj and Swami Dayanand's writings. I asked my father about my grandfather's exact age at the time of his 'conversion'. My father shrugged his shoulders and said: 'Pata nahi. Maine kabhi pooccha hi nahi.' Don't know, I never asked. I guess the question of when my grandfather became Arya Samaji was irrelevant from my father's perspective because he was born into the Arya Samaj and regarded it as being intrinsic to his family. For my grandfather, the Hindu identity supplanted his narrower—caste (Baniya) and sectarian (Vaishnava)—identity because he saw the former as a more capacious and inclusive identity that promised equality, challenged the authority of the Brahmins, and stood against superstition, ritualism, and religious bigotry. The

Hindu identity was also a 'majoritarian' identity. That is, it rested on the belief that the Hindus were in the majority in India and therefore entitled to primacy in social and political spheres. And above all, this identity was forged in service of the nation. It stood in defiance of British and Western values. The inescapable allure of this identity also came from its claim of being sanatan. Hinduism, as defined by Dayanand, was a civilization and not just a religion. Bharat was the cradle of this civilization. And this civilization had time and again weathered attacks by foreigners and yet endured. The Arya Samaj thus offered a new community—radical, modern, and nationalistic—that carried immense appeal. My grandfather embraced it with pride and élan. At some point he even dropped his caste surname and became a Vedic—the Aryan.

3

THE COW PROTECTION MOVEMENT

Dayanand and after him the Arya Samaji publicists vigorously undertook the setting up of gaurakshini sabhas and gaushalas, cow protection societies and cow shelters across North India. However, they were not the first to raise the issue of cow protection. The Sikhs, especially the Kukas or Namdharis, had taken up the issue of cow protection since the 1790s well into the late 1880s. However, the Arya Samaj-led cow protection movement that originated in the 1880s was exceptional in the way it brought together different ideological groups, urban-rural politics, and rival caste groups under one umbrella much before Gandhi did. It was successful in rallying all shades of Hindus—radical reformists, traditionalists, and the ones holding the middle ground. Dayanand's critique of Brahmanical hegemony over the study of the Vedas and the performance of rituals, excessive ritualism, the caste system, and the oppression of women were the main issues that had upset the traditional priestly class who responded by forming sanatan dharma sabhas for the defence of the more ritualized version of Hinduism. In many places the sanatan dharma sabhas were pitted against the local units of the Arya Samaj. However, Arya Samaj's efforts towards cow protection was one issue that diluted the hostile objections of the traditional Hindu priests to Dayanand Saraswati's reformist and iconoclastic attitude.

While the gaurakshini sabha workers of yore did not have access to WhatsApp and the internet for dissemination of their ideas, they nevertheless ingeniously utilized the traditional communication networks. They drew on the roving culture of the ascetics—monks, mendicants, fakirs, sadhus, and sanyasis who were constantly on the move. Like them, they toured different cities of Punjab, Uttar Pradesh, Bengal, and Bihar energizing the cow protection movement. By the 1890s, they had reached Sind, Rajputana, Dacca, Bombay, and Madras. They used the local melas or fairs and festivals, storytelling and oral traditions (kathas, bhajans, poems, songs and speeches), the touring troupes that recited and enacted the Ramayana, local theatre performances, and the traffic of pilgrims moving from one place to the other—all the networks that wove in and out of the rural landscape and connected the villages to nearby townships and cities for spreading their message.

The members of the gaurakshini sabha were able to achieve unprecedented mass mobilization by bringing the politics of the urban centres closer to the rural hinterland. The urban sabha members utilized the existing organizational networks of other Hindu organizations to popularize the movement in the villages. In many instances, prominent rural leaders and landowners lent support and facilitated the sabha workers as embracing a movement around the cow helped maintain their hold over peasantry. The rural folk attending the gaurakshini sabha events were asked to bring a chutki, a handful of rice, as membership fee which was later reclaimed for money that went towards providing for the gaushalas or for the upkeep of the publicists. The movement offered people the opportunity to participate in different ways. They could help set up a gaushala, go from village to village for fundraising, donate money for marriages and feasts, copy and relay chain letters publicizing cow protection, or help in the circulation of books and pamphlets.

The cow protection movement was unique in the way it transformed the nature of rural protest by temporarily dissolving rural factionalism and bringing rival caste groups into a coalition. One sees an instance of this in the cow protection movement in eastern Uttar Pradesh during the 1890s. The rural leadership comprised lower subordinate officials such as the postmasters, judicial clerks, and kanungos who oftentimes came from land-owning castes and wealthier tenants/peasants (such as Bhuinhars and Thakurs) or were Brahmin schoolmasters (Tiwaris and Dubes) whose interests did not always converge and could be mutually opposed except when agitating for cow protection. All of them, in turn, exploited the existing fissures in rural society between different social groups and drew on their caste, kinship, and patron-client network for mobilization. A socio-historical context with a predominance of Brahmanical theology (with its emphasis on the cow) and the Vaishnavite Krishna cult also made the soil fertile for such a mobilization.

The cow protection movement also inventively used the thriving visual and print culture of books, journals, magazines, pamphlets, handbills, posters, cartoons, chapbooks, and newspapers for publicizing its cause. By the second half of the nineteenth century, printing had grown into a big industry with a network of ancillary industries involved in manufacturing printing machines, paper, and dyes that were used for printing; and once printed, for distribution and circulation of the material in different forms. The low-cost mass printing of images (paintings, photographs, drawings, cartoons, and religious art) gave further impetus to the vigorous print culture. The Naval Kishore Press at Lucknow, Sri Venkateshwar Press, and the Raja Ravi Varma Press in Bombay were some of the printing presses at the forefront of the print revolution. Print created a new public culture of debate, dialogue, and controversies akin to social media today. Different communities were printing and disseminating their religious texts, opinions of their leaders, and propaganda materials. There was equal room for divergent opinions and ideas contesting each other to circulate.

The generations from the late nineteenth century onwards grew up immersed in this print culture, encountering it at news stands, railway bookstalls, road intersections, outside schools, colleges, temples, and hospitals, at religious fairs and festivals; and as pocket-sized images that people could carry in their wallets or stick or hang on the walls of their homes or keep in the family altar. The printed material circulated rapidly because it was cheap and portable. Even poor people could afford calendars and cheap prints to decorate their homes. The use of everyday spoken languages also made the printed word accessible to a wide cross section of society. From the ones who could read to the ones who could not read—the latter could hear it being read aloud. Printing created new avenues of mass dissemination of information about everything under the sun. It also enabled mass education with the publication of school texts, children's books and the growth of a new culture of school and public libraries. It allowed sections of the population such as children, women, the poor, and the lower castes to participate, engage, and have a voice in the public sphere as new forms of literature such as novels, autobiographies, journals, and magazines evolved. Access to reading and writing books changed social relations, engendered new ideological struggles, and transformed peoples' consciousness. Hereon books became a testament to the power of the printed word, a form of encoding human thought that couldn't easily be erased.

Under the influence of the Nagari Pracharini Sabha of Banaras (1893) and the Hindi Sahitya Sammelan of Allahabad (1910) that established an ancient ancestry for the Hindi language going back to Sanskrit, Hindi became the vehicle for spreading the message of gauraksha. Many tracts and magazines such as *Gausewak, Gaudharma Prakash, Bharat Dimdima Natak, Gaumata ka Sandesh* eulogizing the cow and the need for cow protection came into circulation. Alongside the image of the gaumata, the cow as the mother of all Hindus, was mass produced and consumed. In these images, the body of the cow was presented as a repository of all Hindu gods, eighty-four of them. Tucked away in the corner of these images (see image on p. 36) was the figure of a villainous butcher depicted as a wild boar (on top of the image is inscribed: kalyugi mansahari jeevon ko dekho, see the meat-eaters of kaliyug) who in order to satiate his lust for cow meat was poised to recklessly annihilate the sacred symbol of the Hindus. The dharmaraj, upholder of dharma, a Hindu man is shown begging the butcher for mercy saying 'mat maro gaye sarv ka jeevan hai', don't kill the life-giving cow that serves all. The 'all' here refers to the national community sitting below the cow's belly waiting to receive cow milk—the Hindus (three male figures—a reference to the dvija, the three twice-born castes of the Brahmana, Kshatriya, and Vaishya), and a single image of a Parsi, a Christian, and a Muslim man. This was the image of the Indian nation capacious enough to include Hindus, Muslims, Christians, and Parsis.

Chaurasi Devtaon ki Gai,
made by Anant Shivaji Desai, printed
by Raja Ravi Varma Press, Bombay

In other images the gaumata, the giver of milk that nourished the Hindu body was presented as a suffering mother who beseeched and invoked her Hindu son's manliness and sense of pride to save her life and honour. Or a woman is shown waiting patiently with a bowl for cow's milk while the calf suckled at her udders reminiscent of Dayanand's injunction not to milk the cow until a few months after giving birth to a calf. Thus Hindu selfhood came to be intimately tied to the protection of the cow in relation to the rogue Muslim who insisted on eating beef and spoke Urdu (a language that was considered as the effeminate language of dancing girls and prostitutes). The relentless endurance of these images in the popular domain is attested by the fact that this image first appeared in Azamgarh district in 1894, then reappeared in the Hindi journal *Madhuri* in 1937, and then again in the 1960s as a calendar image, and thence made its way to family altars and knick-knacks like coin boxes in most homes in northern India, and can now be found easily on the internet.

It seems that by the late nineteenth century, the Hindu Khatiks or butchers did not undertake even the tanning of cow or buffalo hide. Although one doesn't know conclusively how far back in history the Hindu Khatik's aversion to handling cows went (or whether it can be attributed to the influence of Vaishnavism or to the Arya Samaj publicists) it was quite likely that it was primarily the Kasais, Muslim butchers, who were handling cattle in northern India in this period. The spectre of the Muslim butcher, the Kasai, was thus born. It was an image of the rapacious Other who possessed the meanest traits that one wanted to distance oneself from. It was as if the Hindu had projected all his worst fears on to the Muslim Other. The traits that the Muslim was believed to possess existed because the Hindu imagined them to be there. The Muslim thus became both an object of fear and a curious attraction. He possessed one trait, in particular, that the Hindu hated him for. This was the Muslim's sexual potency. What else could account for the religiously-sanctified polygamy. A collection of essays titled *Humara Bhishan Haas* (Our Severe Decline) stated:

> Our sexually unsatisfied widows are especially prone to Muslim hands and by producing Muslim children, they increase their numbers and spell disaster for the Hindus...You yourselves say, would you like our Aryan widows to read '*nikah*' with Muslims?

Perhaps the sexual potency of the Muslim man was an element that rendered the Hindu inadequate and insecure of his own potency. Evidence from the period shows the Hindu wished he possessed the Muslim's sexual abilities or prowess; the Muslim was hated for having it. And this made the Hindu fearful for his women (wives, mothers, daughters, sisters, and gaumata) who were seen as objects of Muslim lust. As one pamphlet titled *Chand Musalmano ki Harkatein* [The Deeds of Few Muslims] stated:

> Ai Aryon kyon so rahe ho pair pasare
> Muslim ye nahi honge humare tumhare...
> Muslim banane ke liye scheme banayi...
> Ekkon ko gali gaon mein le kar ghoomte hain.

Parde ko daal Muslim aurat ko baithate hain.

Aye Aryans, why do you sleep with legs spread out
These Muslims will not be yours or ours...
In order to convert to Islam they made a cunning
scheme...
They roam in streets and villages sitting in carts,
Behind the veil they make Muslim women sit

The last line was a reference to the abduction of Hindu women by Muslim carriage drivers in order to satisfy their lust and to convert them to Islam.

The Muslim, they argued, did not stop at stealing their women and cows but was also gunning for lower-caste Hindus and untouchables by means of conversion. The cow protectionists thus came to be deeply involved in combating propaganda programs for the conversion of Dalit communities by Christian missionaries and Muslim organizations in the early twentieth century. For instance, the Muslim organizations primarily targeted the lower castes in various towns of Uttar Pradesh for conversion. Christian missionaries were able to convert several sweepers, Chandals, Chamars, Doms, and Lai Begis. The publicists of the Arya Samaj and the Hindu Mahasabha lamented these conversions as they felt the Hindu 'numbers were declining' and launched a massive campaign against Christian and Muslim conversion. As one propaganda poem stated:

Hota nahin anar kabhi amrud badal ke.
Tab hindu kis bhanti aaj bhaye muslim dal ke...
Brahman, kshatri, vaishya, kshetra mein aage awo,

Antyaj bandhu samaj vishad saadar apnavo...
Teli nai khatik tamoli bhaat bhikhari,

dhobi dhanuk lodh bodh se baarho agari
Kurmi kevat kuril jati ke kori bhangi, aasha tumhin
se lagi bano sache sangi.

A pomegranate can never change into a guava.
Then how can Hindus today become a part of the
Muslim community?
Brahmins, Kshatriyas, Vaishyas, please come forward,
accept with respect your junior brothers
March ahead oil miller, barber, vegetable seller, bard,
beggar, washerman, cotton-carder.
Kurmi, boatman, Kuril, sweeper—we have faith in
you, become our true associates.

गेंद फेंकने वाला देखो, गेंद उठाने वाला देख !
एक जाति के ये दोनों थे, इसकी भी ओर मन में देख !

जो ईसाई बन जाता है, वह चहूल का देखो रह !
जो हिन्दू है उसके जूता सीने का भी देखो ढह !!

Converted and unconverted Dalits

The caption of the left image reads: See the one playing ball and the one picking it up! They once belonged to the same caste, please pay attention to that!

The caption of the right image reads: See the colour of the untouchable who becomes a Christian! See the manner of stitching the shoe of the one who is Hindu!!

The above image is from the popular Hindi publication *Chand* with an upper-caste readership. These caricatures generally depicted two kinds of Dalit men—converted and unconverted—or two Dalit women. The converted Dalit man was more masculine, had a confident gait, was well-dressed, wore shoes, and was more European-like in the activities he was engaged in (playing tennis or ordering the servants about or walking like a sahib or flaunting his wealth). The unconverted man was shown engaged in a menial task, physically feeble, poorly dressed, barefoot, and smaller in size. There was a general belief that conversion brought about the stark physical and material elevation of the Dalits. These caricatures of Dalit men were an acknowledgement of the benefits that accrued to the Dalits as result of conversion and were also meant to serve as a warning to the upper castes that they were fast losing their lower-caste Hindu brethren to Christianity (unless they did something about it).

The Arya Samaj workers also started contact programs to win the lower castes over to the 'Hindu' side. The lower castes that had hitherto been barred entry or participation in upper-caste homes and festivities were now invited despite their highly 'impure' status. The image on p.42 extols the efforts to establish equality with lower caste.

A close examination of the image shows a Brahmin and an

पानी की प्यास

गाड़ी छूटनेमें दो मिनटकी देरी है, पंडितजी और घिसुवा साथ-ही-साथ नलसे पानी ले रहे हैं ।

The Thirst for Water:
It's two minutes for the train to leave,
Panditji and Ghisuva are together taking water from the tap

untouchable drawing water together. However, they are not actually taking water from the same tap. Note that the taps are separate and there is no physical contact between the two. This neither liquefied the untouchable's identity nor sullied the ritual purity of the Brahmin. Moreover, once brought into the Hindu fold, the attempt was to wean the lower castes away from the consumption of beef and to acquire the values and ways of the upper castes. This was shuddhi or purification of the hitherto polluted castes to ensure the integrity of the Hindu self and their numerical majority.

Although several Brahmins opposed shuddhi of the lower castes, most of the leading Hindi newspapers and magazines such as *Abhyudaya*, *Chand*, and *Sudha* lauded the efforts of the Hindu organizations.

The converts could now take part in a new Arya Samaj-sponsored piety that was captivating and all-absorbing. They could perform havan (fire sacrifice), wear the janeyu (sacred thread), sing bhajans, participate in updesh (sermons), observe sandhya (morning and evening prayers), and above all read the *Satyarth Prakash*, a holy text which they had hitherto been denied access to. Consequently, the Arya Samaj brought several communities, local deities, and cults under its influence. The Gogapir was one such cult to get absorbed. The appeal of the Gogapir cult that had undergone Rajputization in the seventeenth century and had come to be associated with Brahmanical rituals of worship in the nineteenth century was significantly diminished by the twentieth century as the Jats and Bishnois came under the influence of Arya Samaj. New, low-priced hagiographical material in the form of *Goga Puran* and *Goga Chalisa* along with calendars and posters with Goga in the company of Hindu gods began to circulate during pilgrimage fairs. The deity's higher status also meant an increase in the number of followers from upper-caste communities and the glossing over of the taboo associated with local and lower-caste cults. This appropriation thus opened up the 'Hindu' identity to the traditional followers of Gogapir who began to worship gods that they had hitherto considered 'Hindu'.

This Hindu universalism became a mighty juggernaut

that helped mobilize several lower-caste groups, untouchable communities, and women's groups for the nationalist cause. The 'Hinduising process' of the colonial state (the census, representation, and electoral politics) also aided the process. New origin myths of the lower caste, such as the Chuhras who went from being farmers and agricultural labourers to sweepers belonging to the Balmiki community, were forged. The myths assigned them status within the varna system (in the golden age of Aryans) and blamed their fallen status on the period of Muslim rule. Similar was the case of the Jats, the peasant-pastoral community of North India who were organized around anti-Brahmanical ideas but eventually contributed to the strengthening of Hindu orthodoxy. In fact, for the Jats, being Aryan meant being a Hindu warrior, a Kshatriya. The appeal of being an Aryan thus lay in its offer of a militant and muscular Hindu collective identity. This identity in time became a call to arms.

The Islamic identity of the Muslim converts also began to change by the nineteenth century. What was earlier a nominal commitment gradually started becoming more 'total'. Sporadic reformist movements advocating a more normative practice of Islam had begun to emerge from the late seventeenth century onwards but it was only in the nineteenth century that they began to acquire greater following for their unitary reformist vision. It was primarily the changes in transportation technology that enabled greater travel opportunities for the Hajj to Mecca; and growth in circulation of Quranic literature enabled converts to become more aware of the gap between the commandments and the practice of religion. Islam began to be slowly seen as a unified set of absolute norms that believers must adhere to. The cultural Arabization of Indian Islamic practices and the rise of the Pakistan movement were the two direct outcomes of this reformist impulse. Stoking the incipient Islamic universalism's growth in India was the simultaneous rise of Hindu universalism.

Hereby began a gradual process of erosion of a long and deep history of pluralist and composite religio-cultural traditions. The belief that Hindu and Muslim communities were completely separate, antagonistic, and had an exclusive and autonomous heritage with no shared history did not sprout overnight. It was a process that took several decades to take root. This is not to say that differences and conflicts between the two communities were unknown in pre-British history but there also existed deep intra-community and sectarian conflict between the Shias and Sunnis; and between the Vaishnavites, the Shaivites and the different sects or sampradayas identifying themselves as Hindu. Although it was by no means completely successful in erasing the multiple traditions that had existed, the Arya Samaj accentuated the existing differences by offering a new way of belonging.

VIOLENCE FORGES COMMUNITY

The Arya Samaj also offered an opportunity to participate in collective action around gauraksha. Participation in group resistance where individuals came together and collectively opposed the sale or slaughter of cows was a new experience. These were people who otherwise might have had nothing more than marketplace cordiality binding them on an ordinary day. Now together they intercepted the cows in transit, marched for hours in the thousands to prevent slaughter on Bakra Eid (the Islamic festival in which cows and goats are sacrificed), defied British officials, chanted slogans, mobilized people from neighbouring villages, gheraoed Muslim neighbourhoods, and in some instances participated in violence. The physical act of crowding together generated a sense of possessing primordial kinship that actually might never have existed. The bodies pressing together and breathing in unison bred a new kind of self-identification where everyone became one with the other in the crowd. It also engendered a new kind of belonging, a sense of shared state of mind, and one impelled by a thirst and hunger for attaining one's purpose.

The local people who did not participate directly in the violent agitation got drawn into it when they shielded the participants by hiding them in their homes or by keeping silent when the local police officer came knocking at their door or passing on information from house to house or hoarding lathis and swords for the agitators. People living further away from the locality of the riot also got sucked into its vortex through news that now travelled speedily through a network of railways, telegraph, and print that morphed into rumours and gossip in no time. They talked about the anti-cow-killing agitation sitting under the village tree, the elders gathered at the chowk discussed the ramifications, women exchanged the news as they went to fetch water from the well, travellers on buses and trains swapped notes about the recent developments, hawkers sold newspapers by shouting out headlines of the riot, tonga-drivers gossiped with townspeople as they drove back and forth, postmen delivering mail and milkmen doing rounds of houses did their part to broadcast the latest news. This was not the first time that rumours had mobilized Indians. Several decades ago, the rumours of greased cartridges and flour mixed with crushed animal bones had led to a rebellion in sepoy ranks, shaking the British Raj to its roots.

This was the affective community of violence. A community bound by emotions that arose out of participating in, experiencing, witnessing, telling stories of, and exchanging news of violence. The power of violence lay in its ability to alter human reality so radically that people temporarily annulled all connection with any reality other than the one generated by violence. This new reality was then retrospectively projected back on all the preexisting realities dyeing them all in the colour of the present. Thus began the process of forging Hindu and Muslim identities as separate and historically antagonistic for at least the people involved with and affected by the anti-cow-killing riots. It spawned one homogenized master narrative: the fact of the historically violent Muslim, of his excesses and his insatiable lust. The violent conflict around cow protection went a long way towards the creation of community identities that could be invoked as primordial each time there was a conflict.

The energy of the cow protection movement was focused more on the prevention of the sale and slaughter of cows and relatively less on their upkeep. The sale of cows to butchers was prevented through a variety of means—persuasion, economic incentives, coercion, and social boycott. This brought the cow protectionists in conflict with Muslim butchers and lower castes such as the Chamars, Nats, and Banjaras who were involved in the purchase, sale, and transport of cows and in tanning hides and who were also seen as being outside the caste system. These incidents increasingly began to take the form of 'anti-cow-killing' riots, especially around the celebration of Bakra Eid. Research has shown a significant spike in such incidents from 1881 onwards that continued well into the 1920s. This period marks a significant shift in the evolution of the Hindu and the Muslim identities as mutually antagonistic.

The early forms of anti-colonial political mobilization also inadvertently drew on these nascent community identities. Be it the week-long Ganpati festival that Bal Gangadhar Tilak organized in Pune from 1893 onwards, the Swadeshi movement in response to Lord Curzon's Partition of Bengal in 1905, or the public celebration of Durga Puja in Bengal, each drew on ready and widely-shared religious symbols for political mobilization and carried an anti-Muslim tenor. In fact several sanyasis from different monastic traditions and sampradayas entered the nationalist fray from the 1920s onwards.

Swami Sahajanand Saraswati, a Dasnami sanyasi and Kisan Sabha leader who led political movements protesting rural indebtedness and seeking debt moratorium (1934–35) and the Bakasht agitation for tenancy rights (1936–39) that led to the amendment of the Bihar Tenancy Act (1937) and the Bakasht Lands Act (1938); Baba Ram Chandra, who rose to become the leader of Kisan Sabha in Uttar Pradesh in the 1920s; and Sanyasi Bhawani Dayal, an Arya Samaji associate of Gandhi in Transvaal were some of them. For these sanyasis, social and political activism was an extension of their religious philosophies ranging from Vaishnavism to the writings of Swami Dayanand. So what had started out in the nineteenth century as an internal cultural dialogue, focused on the need to come up with an alternative identity in the colonial context, gradually became a need for solidarity against British colonialism; and by the early twentieth century became the founding stones of nationalist mobilization.

This was not a simple 'politicization of religion', a phrase that has come to dominate the way people understand the relationship between religion and politics. This phrase conveys a simplistic understanding where politics is seen as despoiling the purity of religion. It refers to an instrumentalist use of religion towards nefarious ends. Conceived in this way, it presents religion as existing in a pure realm untarnished by human agency and politics as being this-worldly and a product of baser human emotions and actions. However, this understanding ignores the fundamental political character of religion. Religion has always been political and politics has rarely ever not drawn on religion, its symbols or its vocabulary. They have always shared a symbiotic relationship. Religion, its sites, symbols, and congregations provided an easy constituency (given the potential it had of appealing to a majority of Indian population) and therefore the nationalist leaders drew on them for spreading the anti-colonial message.

The British administrators took a cautious approach to the 'anti-cow-killing' agitation. They saw the agitation and the ensuing violence as a law and order problem but were also keenly aware of it being a threat to their rule. In some places, the violence had been directed not just towards the Muslim community but also towards the local British officers. The British were therefore cautious in their approach as they did not want to be the targets of Hindu retaliation. When it came to the religious identities of the 'peoples' of the Indian subcontinent, the British liked to see themselves as sanctifying a preexistent reality and not as creating one. Nothing could have been further from the truth. They were quietly but radically altering the social reality of the subcontinent. In their view, the difference and the conflict between Hindus and Muslims was not a problem of recent origin but one going far back into history. It encapsulated their view of India as a land of religious bigotry and as possessing a fundamentally irrational character. Religious conflict was a pathological condition and one that was endemic to the Indian subcontinent. This view informed the British introduction of a religion-based census in 1880 that instituted communal enumeration; and the creation of separate electorates in 1909, which granted formal recognition to the minorities in the legislatures. The latter provision was premised on the belief that the conflicts between Hindus and Muslims were of such magnitude that no democratic framework could possibly resolve them. This was a deliberate channelization of electoral politics into religious forms. The main aim was to keep Indian politics fragmented within communities in order to keep the unitary state under their control.

The British officials' reticence in passing laws against cow slaughter reflected their cautious attitude. They believed that the Hindu 'passion for the cow' was ancient and the non-consumption of beef an essential aspect of Hindu identity and therefore left it to the courts to pass judgment. For instance, in his reminiscences of life in India, *Rambles and Recollections of an Indian Official* (1844), W. H. Sleeman, a British administrator and accomplished linguist, gives details of an incident where a cow was slaughtered, despite the local priest's entreaties against it, for feeding British troops. Apparently, this led to the outbreak of 'cholera morbus' in their camps. Sleeman reports another incident where cow slaughter and beef-eating near the Narmada River led to the destruction of the wheat crop and other calamities and diseases in the area. Vincent Smith, a British Indologist and historian credited with writing books on Ashoka and Akbar, annotated the 1915 edition of Sleeman's book. Smith writes in his annotation regarding the beef-eating incident that the local people later witnessed that the trees to which beef was tied slowly withered away. According to him, the Hindu venerated the cow with the sort of passion and intensity that utilitarian explanations (i.e. the arguments based on economic rationality) failed to capture. The only ethnographic account in his view that grasped the Hindu's devotion for the cow was William Crooke's compilation of Indian folklore.

One would imagine that the unifying ideology of the cow protection movement gave it longevity and success in achieving an all-India legal ban on cow slaughter. However, the success of the movement in this sphere was limited. The British held on to a policy of neutrality which in time tilted towards the Muslims and ultimately they suppressed the movement by breaking its organizational spine and stamping out its communication networks. Restricting the cow slaughter movement's success (although there were instances of anti-cow-slaughter riots in Bombay and Rangoon as well) was the fact that it developed primarily in the context of North India and disregarded the socio-historical context of north-eastern and southern India. In these areas Hinduism was in dialogue with not only Islam but Christianity and Judaism and there existed less squeamishness with regard to the consumption of beef. But more on that later.

Interestingly, when it came to the colonial courts and

the magistrates passing judgments regarding upholding or banning cow slaughter, there was no uniform or consistent pattern. Historians have described the situation as one of judicial anarchy. For instance, cow-killing was banned in Mathura in 1805 but was soon resumed in full knowledge of the magistrate. In the town of Mau it was banned in 1806 and then reversed in 1863 and reinstated in a year's time. In fact it was the High Court judgment of the North Western Provinces in 1888 that was instrumental in galvanizing the cow protection movement. It stated that the 'cow' was not a sacred object and Muslims were not offending Hindu sensibilities if they were slaughtering the animal. The lack of state protection meant that individual Arya Samaj activists took it upon themselves to carry out the 'sacred work' of cow protection. In 1893, cow slaughter was judicially curtailed in Bareilly and in Ayodhya in 1915. In Punjab, the beef trade was regulated and slaughter was confined to municipal abattoirs in 1890 but concessions were made for Eid where Muslims were allowed to slaughter cows in their homes. In 1919, the government issued a circular stating that cow slaughter should be allowed where it was customary. However, this was already the practice being followed in most places. In the princely states ruled by Hindu and Sikh rulers, cow slaughter was consistently seen as a crime carrying exemplary punishments. Even the import of beef for sale was prohibited in some states. However, in states with Muslim rulers there was no uniform practice. In some it was prohibited and permitted in others. Irrespective of administrative prohibitions or permissiveness there existed a wide gap between administrative policies and actual practice on the ground.

Even after India's independence, cow slaughter has come under legal regulation in the majority of Indian states but has not been completely banned. The Constituent Assembly after hotly debating whether there should be a constitutional ban on cow slaughter in all of India finally included an article on cow slaughter in the Directive Principles of State policy (DPSP) that were meant to guide the state in policy-making. However, unlike fundamental rights, the articles of DPSP were not enforceable in a court of law. The article on cow slaughter was couched in the vocabulary of scientific organization of animal husbandry and primarily upheld the sanctity of the cow as an economically useful milch animal (much in the way Dayanand had). People saw the insertion of this article as a compromise between constitutional secularism and Hindu majoritarianism. The variation between administrative policies and ground realities of the kind that had existed under the British Raj continued in post-Independence India. By the 1950s, under the pressure of electoral politics, cow slaughter was banned in Bihar, Uttar Pradesh, Rajasthan, and Madhya Pradesh. Individuals and social groups have continued to legally challenge the ban on cow slaughter on grounds of the violation of right to freedom of religion and right to freedom of trade and occupation. The Supreme Court of India in turn has repeatedly upheld (in 1958 and again in 2005) the cattle slaughter ban as constitutional. However, on 11 July 2017, the Supreme Court stepped away from its earlier stand by suspending the ban on sale of cows for slaughter. The court's order was in response to the central government's ban on the sale of cattle (and cows) for slaughter on 25 May 2017. The politico-legal tussle continues as the majority of Indian states (except Kerala, West Bengal, Arunachal, Mizoram, Meghalaya, Nagaland, Tripura, and Sikkim) have banned the sale/slaughter of cows and cattle (in some form or other).

The major success of the twentieth century cow protection mobilization thus primarily lay in forging a new Hindu identity—a community that was united in its belief of the cow's sacredness and the urgent need to protect it. Around this identity developed a 'discourse,' that is, a set of beliefs, attitudes, ways of being, vocabulary and practices where cow protection and the non-consumption of beef came to mark the boundary between the Hindu self and the Muslim Other who ate beef and spoke Urdu. This identity situated anyone consuming beef as not only outside the Hindu fold but also antagonistic to it (as anti-Hindu). This discourse was the cow protection movement's indelible legacy. Lending strength to the Hindu identity was not only evidence from the ancient Shastras (as culled out by Dayanand) that prohibited cow killing but also colonial ethnography that established the Hindu identity as 'sanatan'. That is, it was eternal, imperishable, primordial, and continually flowing from India's ancient past to its modern present. It was also a resurgent identity that had withstood the ravages of time and the depredations of foreign aggressors: the Greeks, Muslims and now the British. Scrubbed clean of the dust and grime of centuries, it shone as a bright beacon calling out to the faithful to congregate in order to reclaim and protect what rightfully belonged to them. This identity erased any instance of beef-eating in the Indian subcontinent's history except when done by the Muslim and the outcaste Other. Once this discourse seeped into the public psyche it became easy to mobilize people for rashtriya chetna, national consciousness, where the nation was defined as Hindu. Vinayak Damodar Savarkar was to take this baton forward when he became the president of the Hindu Mahasabha in 1937.

A young man who responded to Savarkar's clarion call of the 'Hindu rashtriya chetna' was my grandfather. His path to the Hindu Mahasabha was paved through the Arya Samaj. His father and he were born and brought up in the city of Indore. They say the year my grandfather's family migrated to Indore there was a famine in Rajasthan. They had come to Indore in the hope of finding work and starting a new life. At the time, the city of Indore was the capital of the Maratha clan of Holkars and a bustling trade centre specializing in grains, textiles, and stock-market betting. The city had not remained untouched by the gaurakshini sabha's mobilization. The late nineteenth century British records talk about how the Baniya community of Indore comprising moneylenders and traders was at the forefront of the cow protection movement and prevented the sale of cows to butchers. In 1890, they are said to have begun to pressure the Holkar maharaja to patronize and support the movement. Much to the annoyance of the British officials, the Baniya community prevailed over the maharaja because of their financial clout. They controlled the city's commercial life and also gave the Holkars cash advances for taking care of their administrative expenses.

Although I doubt that the memory of this incident was alive by the time my grandfather embraced the Arya Samaj, he was very devoted to the cause of gauraksha.

One morning as I stood at the kitchen counter cutting an apple for my son's school tiffin, all of a sudden I had the answer to why my grandfather had passed on Bharmall's story to me, one of his oldest grandchildren. I knew the significance that the remembrance of Bharmall's valour held for his present. It had been in front of my eyes all this time but it was only now that I was seeing it, nay witnessing it. The air around me became very still. Several images raced and danced in front of my eyes all seamlessly connected. It was a radiating vision, a radiant tableau. I saw my septuagenarian grandfather looking luminous with the flowing white beard that he had grown after becoming a vanaprasthi. The books that my grandfather had given me to read as a child swam past with their pages fluttering. The gauraksha handbills that he printed and distributed floated past me and through the kitchen window. I heard the mooing of the buffaloes and cows in their pen in my grandfather's backyard. The clanging of the small iron board hanging on the front gate of our Indore house which announced that cow urine was available for free, gau mutra nishulk uplabdh hai. I felt the heat of the crackling flames of the sacred fire as my husband and I went around it seven times with a female Sanskrit professor (not a male priest) tying us in holy matrimony. I could hear my grandfather bending over and asking the professor in all earnestness if he could gift a cow as part of my dowry. My family's displeasure at my starting to eat eggs because although I was vegetarian I was no longer 'pure'. I heard my grandfather explaining to a friend why he had sent his eldest son to Delhi for higher studies: 'Maine apne bade bete ko desh ki seva ke liye de diya hai'. I had sacrificed myeldest son for the service of the nation. I could hear his tirade against Gandhi for having given compensation to Pakistan as my brother and I lay nestled in his armpit. His naming my cousins Shivaji and Savarkar. My chacha's liking for guns. My husband and I laughing loudly as we heard my father innocently ask his younger brother who sat there twirling his moustache why he spent so much money on buying guns and whether he intended to use them for killing the mice in the house. The sound of the pen scratching against paper as my grandfather wrote pamphlets warning Hindus that if they didn't watch out they would soon be outnumbered and beaten by the Muslims and that Mother Teresa was 'nark ka farishta', prophet of hell. He had dropped the caste surname but wore the janeyu, the sign of being a dvija. For him, the Arya Samaj, cow protection, the nation, and his self had come together in Bharmall's story. Jagdish, my grandfather, was negotiating his present through this story. He saw Bharmall not just as his ancestor but himself in Bharmall. Jagdish Prasad was Bharmall. Bharmall was a link in the chain that tied Jagdish to the Aryans. They were all warriors, the dharmaraj, who had devoted their lives to protect the sanatan parampara, the eternal tradition. By telling me Bharmall's story he had passed on the parampara's baton. I had been anointed as the next in line. The knife I was cutting the apple with nicked my thumb. I dropped the knife and sucked hard at the thumb to stop the blood from flowing.

A gauraksha handbill

|| ओ३म् ||

मदर टेरेसा, नर्क का फरिश्ता

क्रिस्टोफर हिचेंस द्वारा 'नर्क का फरिश्ता' नामक फिल्म का निर्माण कर बी.बी.सी. लंदन के माध्यम से प्रदर्शन किया गया। इस फिल्म में गरीबों की मसीहा, करूणा और मातृत्व की साक्षात मूर्ति कहलाने वाली मदर टेरेसा का यह वीभत्स दृश्य देखकर दर्शक अचंभित हो गये।

फिल्म में दिखाया गया कि मदर टेरेसा का सेवा केन्द्र जहां रोगियों को स्ट्रेचर पर लिटा कर ही रखा जाता है। इन रोगियों को बीमारी ठीक होने की दवा नहीं दी जाती है। किंतु ऐसी दवाई दी जाती है जिससे रोगियों के शरीर में ऐसी पीड़ा होती है जो सहनशक्ति के बाहर होती है। देखने वाले यह समझें कि रोगियों को बहुत कष्ट हो रहा है और इन दुखी रोगियों का मदर टेरेसा के सेवा केन्द्र में इलाज हो रहा है किंतु सेवा केन्द्र में भर्ती होने वाले रोगियों को इलाज करवाने के लिये अस्पताल नहीं भेजा जाता। यह प्रतीक्षा की जाती है कि रोगी जल्दी से जल्दी मर जावें।

फिल्म निर्माता क्रिस्टोफर हिचेंस ने लंदन के गार्जियन सामाहिक समाचार पत्र १३ नवंबर १९९३ के अंक में लेख लिखा, कि मदर टेरेसा सेवा नहीं सेवा के नाम पर व्यापार करती हैं और अमेरिका तथा अनेक समाचार पत्रों के मालिक राबर्ट मेक्सवेल से सेवा के लिये धन प्राप्त करती हैं। वह धन कहाँ है? जबकि धन रोगियों की सेवा के लिये मिलता है। इस सेवा केन्द्र पर सेवा तो नहीं की जाती है। केवल यह बताया जाता है कि रोगियों का इलाज किया जाता है।

समाचार पत्र 'दि लासेट' के संपादक ने लिखा है कि मदर टेरेसा सेवा के नाम पर व्यापार करती हैं। रोगियों का इलाज करने के बजाय उनकी लाशों पर प्रार्थना करती हैं। पाठकगण, मदर टेरेसा सेवा के नाम पर हिन्दू को ईसाई बनाने का कार्य करती रही हैं। नागालैंड, मिजोरम, अरूणाचल, मेघालय, सिक्किम, त्रिपुरा, मणीपुर आदि प्रांतों में मदर टेरेसा की नकली सेवा से ९०% हिन्दू ईसाई बनाये जा चुके हैं। ये सब ईसाई ही नहीं बन गये हैं। भारतीय संस्कृति, सभ्यता एंव राष्ट्र विरोधी बन गये हैं।

The pamphlet on Mother Teresa

5

THE INVISIBILITY OF VIOLENCE

We arrived in Khatu Shyamji on a cool summer morning. The sun had just come out and was warming the temple canopies. This was my second trip to Khatu Shyamji with my husband and a friend. In all these years of marriage, shifting houses, moving continents, changing jobs, becoming a parent and raising a family, the dusty storeroom of memories had grown. Memories that comforted and delighted but also gnawed and haunted. These memories were like boggarts— the shapeshifters that lurk in the darkest recesses of one's soul and are continuously changing form. They were about remembrance but as much as about forgetting. My first trip to Khatu Shyamji with my grandfather was one such shapeshifting memory. I had completely forgotten that my mother had accompanied us on that trip until I saw a photo that a cousin had mined for the slideshow for her memorial service. Disconcerted, I gaped at the photo trying very hard to recall her presence. To my distress nothing came to me. The photographs with my mother posing at Bharmall's shrine and at Khatu's Shymaji Temple scrolled across the screen falsifying my memory and leaving me with a dull ache. By visiting Khatu Shyamji again perhaps I was hoping to relive, retrieve or release this boggart of a memory and create a new one.

On arriving in Khatu, my husband asked me for the directions to Bharmall ka sata. It was only then that I realized I had no idea of its location. The town had been completely transformed in the last two decades. Nor was there a family member whom I could call to check. It took us nearly two hours of going around the town, stopping at numerous places, and asking several people before arriving at the sata. I had wrongly assumed that the shrine was a famous one and that most townspeople would know of it. A kind storekeeper called up and connected us to an octogenarian ex-sarpanch, Bansidhar Sharma, who confirmed the location of the shrine. He had been in correspondence with my grandfather until his passing. On arriving at the sata we saw that some pandit had made the shrine his home and had painted slogans praising Lord Krishna and Lord Ram on its walls. He had no clue of the history of the shrine and was treating it as a temple devoted to Hanuman, the Monkey God. In the middle of the hall was a tablet with a cow and a human figure plastered with the orange paste that is generally used on Hanuman's idols. This was Bharmall and his cow. I stood there with mixed feelings. I wasn't sure what was annoying me more, the lost history or the appropriation of the shrine. Before leaving we took photographs of the shrine to document our visit.

We next visited Sarpanch Bansidhar Sharma's house. He had mentioned on the phone that he was feeling indisposed and therefore didn't wish to leave his house. Sharmaji's son Niranjan Sharma, an advocate, received us and took us to the back of the house where his father's room was located. Sharmaji was indeed taking his afternoon nap. He

Bharmall's shrine

welcomed us and plied us with stories of his association with my grandfather. We sat there listening for about an hour. He told us how the town of Khatu Shyamji was built near a river called Rupavati which has now dried up. The river flowed from east to west. Bharmall indeed lived there and had immolated himself using his yogic powers. He further informed us that my grandfather donated Bharmall's garhi (small fortress) to a charitable trust for making a dharamshala. Another property was donated for setting up a library. Niranjan Sharma joined the conversation after he brought us glasses of lassi. My husband and I were a trifle amused listening to Niranjan who felt that the donations

63

The tablet inside the shrine.
It has faint human and bovine images on it.

my grandfather had made were a huge act of philanthropy as the property would have given our family good financial returns today. Little did he know that it was Bharmall's history that we thought of as our property and not his garhi. It was this intangible family jewel that we had come looking for. As we bid goodbye to the Sharmas with the promise of visiting again, they offered to assist us in installing a tablet narrating Bharmall's story in the shrine.

Our next stop was Khatu's famous Shyamji Temple. The road leading up to the temple was nothing like I remembered. It had burgeoned to unrecognizable proportions. As we stepped inside the temple, the luminous murals on the walls of the inner sanctum came alive depicting scenes from Lord Krishna's life. Krishna, the butter thief, the cowherd, the flute player, the beloved of gopis performing the Raslila, the warrior with the sudarshana chakra, and finally the lord in his viraat roop giving the Gitopadesha to Arjuna. The temple and the town were named after Lord Krishna, also called Shyam for the dark colour of his skin. As we stepped through the silver-covered doors into the garbhagriha, the sanctum sanctorum, we saw an idol with only a head and no body. The head was adorned with a lavish crown and dressed in finery. It appeared like a rock formation that had been later given the form of a head. Such rock formations or fossilized shells known as saligram (salagram or shaligram shila) are worshipped as a form of Vishnu in many temples across India. It is a form of aniconic worship where instead of idols or images, the deity is represented through symbols or objects with no human or animal form.

I collected books and pamphlets about the temple and the town that were being sold at the souvenir and prasad shops that lined the streets that led to the temple. One of them claimed that that there had been continuous worship in the Shyamji Temple since 1720 CE. We were also informed that although the temple was named after Lord Krishna, the idol was of a mythical warrior called Barbareek. Now this was interesting. I hadn't heard of this character. I turned to my

The Shyamji idol

husband who also shook his head. We were intrigued. Why would Barbareek be worshipped and that too as Krishna? Why was he disembodied (or rendered bodiless)? Why was only his head worshipped? What was the religious and symbolic meaning of Barbareek's apotheosis (his elevation to divine status) and the bodiless idol? My research revealed that Barbareek was a character who appeared in the *Skanda Purana* and in the folklore of Telugu, Hindi, and Rajasthani languages and in regions across Kerala, Andhra Pradesh, Orissa, Uttar Pradesh, Rajasthan, Madhya Pradesh, and Nepal. In the *Skanda Purana*, Barbareek is the son of Ghatotkacha, a character from the Mahabharata. Ghatotkacha is Bhima's (the strongest and second oldest of the five Pandavas) son from the demoness Hidimba. Ghatotkacha marries Kaamkantakata (also known as Maurvi) who is the daughter of a ferocious demon named Mur and their son is named Barbareek. In some other tales Barbareek appears as Bhima's son whom he had with Ahilawati who was a Naga kanya, a serpent's daughter. Barbareek appears as Bilalsen in Oriya retellings of Bhima's marriage with Naga kanya. Like most mythological or literary characters Barbareek's story keeps changing in different renditions.

There are also different versions of the story of how Barbareek lost his body. In the *Skanda Purana*, Arjuna boasts that he alone could finish off the Kauravas (the cousins they were at war with) and their army in a day. Barbareek who was present at the time said that he could wipe out the Kauravas in a few seconds. This angered Krishna and he chopped off Barbareek's head with his sudarshan chakra. The Pandavas were stunned and Ghatotkacha ran wailing to Barbareek. Just then fourteen goddesses arrived and recounted the prophecy that Barbareek had to die at the hands of Krishna for his head to be worshipped. Therefore, none should be upset with Krishna for having killed him. Krishna then instructed Devi Chandika to pour divine nectar over Barbareek's head to revive it. Barbareek's head on being revived expressed a desire to watch the battle whereupon Krishna placed

Barbareek's head on a mountaintop. Krishna then blessed Barbareek and said he would be worshipped for as long as the earth, stars, moon, and sun existed.

In another version of the story, Lord Krishna and Arjuna were looking for warriors who could fight the battle with them. On the way they met Barbareek who had three arrows in his quiver. The first arrow could save anything, the second could destroy anything, and the third was to help him distinguish between what could be saved or destroyed. Krishna asked him to demonstrate his prowess by piercing the leaves of all the trees. He pierced all the leaves including a leaf that Krishna had hidden under his foot. Impressed with Barbareek, Krishna wanted to know on which side he planned to fight. Barbareek replied that he was only invincible if he fought on the losing side. Krishna thought that Barbareek would keep switching to the losing side in order to remain invincible and this way the battle would never end. Krishna then requested Barbareek to help him slay a mighty warrior. When Barbareek agreed to do so, Krishna handed him a mirror and asked for the head of the warrior reflected in the mirror. Barbareek realized that he had been tricked but gave his head to Krishna for he was a generous giver. Barbareek was dismayed that he would not be able to see the battle, so Krishna placed his head on a mountaintop to help him witness the battle unhindered.

There are different versions of Barbareek's apotheosis as well. In the first story, he acquires divine status by virtue of his head being cut off by Krishna. In another version, the apotheosis comes after the great battle ends. At the end of the war, when the Pandavas sat around gloating over their victory, and debating the likely causes of their success, Krishna suggested that they consult Barbareek, the talking head on the top of the mountain who was the most objective witness of the battle. When asked, Barbareek responded that in the entire war 'the *Sudarshan Chakra* of the Lord was flying back and forth and Draupadi, the wife of the Pandavas, in the form of goddess *Mahakali* was drinking blood'. Barbareek, thus, declared the might of Krishna and the anger of Draupadi as the prime reasons for the Pandavas' victory. Krishna was delighted by Barbareek's reply and conferred a boon that his head would be worshipped in the Kaliyug as Shyam, one of the names Krishna is known by. This is why the idol in the Shyamji Temple, which is that of Barbareek's head, is worshipped as a symbol of Lord Krishna.

Barbareek's myth is essentially a 'puranic' tale. The earliest Puranas date back to the first century BCE and the composition of the majority of the Puranas is dated to the second to fourth centuries BCE. Although written in the future tense the Puranas describe the political conditions of the times. They are replete with tales and descriptions of foreign invasions, the presence of foreigners, political instability and wars, the killing of women, children, Brahmins, and cows, and stories of the intermixing of races and castes. It is possible that the Barbareek myth is related to the origin of the Rajputs when several tribal communities metamorphosed into kingdoms. The Chandela rulers of Jejakabhukti were one such community who originated in the Central Indian tribal ethnic pool of the Gonds. The primary concern of the rulers

बर्बरीक द्वारा महाभारत युद्ध देखना

Barbareek observing the battle

of these new kingdoms was to establish the legitimacy of their temporal power. They did this essentially by two means. First, by constructing myths about their origin and descent that erased their non-Aryan origins. Secondly, by giving land grants to the Brahmins whose monopoly of religious texts and knowledge gave them the power to sanctify the kingship and obscure the origins of the new rulers. Both these processes had a direct impact on the patronage that the temples received in the region and led to exceptional temple-building activity in this period.

Some distinct aspects which the temple-building activity acquired as a result of this changing nature of society and the creation of new political linkages, was the merging of many local cults into the supra-regional Puranic Hinduism. In a similar vein, Tantric practices began to make their way into Hinduism, Buddhism, and Jainism. The Gogapir in Rajasthan had a similar trajectory of being a non-Aryan deity and later undergoing Rajputization (in the seventeenth century) before being co-opted into the Hindu pantheon in the nineteenth century. Barbareek possibly morphed into Shyamji in a similar manner.

As a myth what does the tale of Barbareek's sacrificing his head and his apotheosis convey? Myths are different from history in that they refer to events and people that are beyond time and memory and may have no existence in the world except in the myth itself. The structure of myths is like that of a symphony. A symphony is composed of several musical units that acquire meaning only in their relationship with each other. There is a narrative and a sense of progression that bind the different units of a symphony. In isolation, the single unit may not have much meaning. Myths may also be likened to a language where different words on their own may just be meaningless sounds but together they acquire meaning. Myths like ballads, genealogies, and folktales perform several functions simultaneously. Myths serve as a way of ordering society's past and anchoring its present in the past. They serve as the society's archives and thus nurture and affirm a society's sense of being. In this much, myths assist in the creation and maintenance of social cohesion. They legitimate social institutions and practices. So how did the Barbareek myth nurture the Aryan society's sense of being? How did it help maintain social cohesion? In what way did it anchor the present in the past?

In Barbareek's name and physiognomy lie the socio-political secret that the myth harbours. The Puranas along with Jain texts and the Mahabharata list Barbaras (Barbareek's namesake) as belonging to the Mleccha tribe. The word Mleccha or barbarian is a pejorative term used for 'foreigners' beyond the pale of the varna system and people living on the extremities of civilization (especially tribes living in forest, coastal, mountain or frontier habitats). The language, physiognomy, customs, and food habits of the Mlecchas were markers of difference. Barbareek was so named for his bushy hair. In the *Skanda Purana*, his father Ghatotkacha says: 'Beta! Tumhaare kesh barbarakaar (ghungrale) hain, isliye tumhara naam Barbareek hoga.' Son! Your hair is Berber-like (curly), your name therefore will be Barbareek. In other folktales Barbareek's hair is likened to snakes (Barbareek ke kesh naag samaan thay). Although he was a son of the Pandavas, Barbareek was not an Aryan. Born of a demoness he had the status of a Rakshas, or demon or a forest-dweller. His hair was a reference to his non-Aryan 'Rakshasa' origins.

The necessary precondition for Barbareek's apotheosis in all the different versions, however, was his sacrifice. In one version, the willing suicide of Barbareek at Krishna's behest makes him the ritual/sacrificial victim (the one who

रणचण्डी हेतु बर्बरीक द्वारा
श्रीकृष्ण भगवान को शीश दान करना।

Barbareek offering his head to Lord Shyam

is sacrificed) but also the one making the offering (the sacrificer). So he is both the ritual victim and the one 'making' the sacrifice. As the sacrificer he is actually substituting for the priest or the god because they are the ones with the ritual status to be the sacrificers. Thus the act of cutting his head confers on him the status enjoyed by the priests and gods. Interestingly, although Barbareek sacrificed his head, it is his body that gets sacrificed. He was allowed to live but without the most potent aspect of his being, that is, his body. It is with his body that Barbareek would have defeated others in battle. So through the act of cutting off his head Barbareek is disembodied but embodied with divine status.

Barbareek's sacrifice ensured that Arjuna's status as the mighty warrior remained unchallenged because had he fought the battle, Barbareek would have upstaged Arjuna. As a ritual victim, Barbareek also served as the surrogate on behalf of his community and prevented the flood of violence that could have engulfed the entire community had Arjuna been eclipsed. So Barbareek's individual sacrifice saved the forest people from the wrath of the Aryans. It deflected the violence away from his community. Barbareek's disembodiment also guaranteed that no children would be born from his loins. The biological perpetuation of the vansha or lineage was a major concern in the story of the Mahabharata. Barbareek's loss of body not only wiped out Bhima's lineage but secured that of Arjuna and Krishna. At the end of the great battle entire generations of sons and grandsons of the Pandavas were wiped out except the little infant Parikshit who was the grandson of Arjuna and Krishna's great-nephew.

The Barbareek myth thus played a dual role: it maintained social cohesion and did so by normalizing or invisibilizing violence. The fact that he was not 'really' killed but continued to exist obviated Krishna's guilt (of beheading him in one version and tricking him into cutting off his head in the other). The victim ultimately is not the victim because he does not get annihilated. As the Rig Veda says: 'You do not really die through this, nor are you harmed. You go on paths pleasant to go on.' For the Lord is divine and therefore sinless, he doesn't suffer the sins of killing; and the act of killing becomes one of sacrifice. The myth thus redeemed Krishna's actions from criminality. Barbareek's sacrifice created a morally pure universe where the Lord is simply the nimitt, the source of liberation. The end goal of acquiring divine status normalized the violence of the beheading. Apotheosis wrote out the violence. Can the myth of Barbareek's apotheosis instead be read as 'Barbareekmedh', the sacrifice of Barbareek?

Barbareek's story is also one of miscegenation—racial intermixing through a sexual relationship. Such unions were socially accepted but never accorded ritual sanctity as they diluted the purity of the Aryan race. A person born out of an Aryan and non-Aryan union was in violation of the order of things. Barbareek's body had to pay the price of this misalliance. Even the etymology of Barbareek's name shows how everyday language, that is, casual words used to describe an individual while appearing not to do so can dispossess the person, erase their identity, their community, and their labour. Words carry a great deal of power as they are mediums for conveying our thought patterns and mental concepts. For instance, the use of words associated with disabilities to describe individuals (retard, lame, blind, pyscho) or community names doubling up as words of abuse (Churha, Chamar, Bhangi) perpetuate deep-seated inequalities. The person of Barbareek, the snake-haired one, thus labelled and marked, was allowed to exist in the Aryan world. He was worshipped not as Barbareek but as Shyam.

The mythological appropriation and co-option within the larger Hindu pantheon erased Barbareek's identity. While his identity is erased his existence is not, it is simply invisibilized. He cannot be annihilated because he and his people were an important resource. If he was exterminated who would cultivate the land, who would guard the forests, who would fight the battles, who would cremate and bury the dead, and who would remove the carcasses of dead cows?

The story of Barbareek is quite similar to that of Eklavya and Karna, two characters from the Mahabharata. Eklavya is a Nishad (a community of forest hunters considered Mleccha) who is asked for his thumb as gurudakshina by Dronacharya to disable him from wielding the bow; Karna is a sutaputra, the son of a chariot-driver (and the illegitimate child of Kunti, mother of the Pandavas) whose armour, the kavach-kundal, is asked for by Lord Indra rendering him defenseless in the battle. Barbareek, Eklavya, and Karna, all had ritually unacceptable birth status or societal location. All three were robbed of what was most precious to them in order to ensure Arjuna remained the mightiest of warriors. But how were their stories written? In the various stories, the historical victims were the Pandavas who had their patrimony taken away by treachery, Krishna whose uncle tried to eliminate him at birth, and Draupadi who was violated by her own. Arjuna was decorated as the meritorious warrior who earned his status through hard work and personal merit; Krishna was anointed as the messenger of peace and the dharmaraj, the protector of dharma; Draupadi's anger annihilated the Kaurava dynasty restoring her honour. However, it was

Barbareek, Eklavya, and Karna who paid the blood price to make Arjuna the mightiest warrior and to avenge Draupadi. In return each was lauded as daanveer, generous and brave givers. It was their good fortune to have had the opportunity to serve the Lord and redeem the stain of low birth. They attained atonement in assisting Arjuna achieve his destiny.

There was yet another way the low-born Other could attain redemption. This was by acquiring the gaze of the dvijas, singing their praises, and by spinning myths of their divinity. Valmiki, the author of the Ramayana, was one such man who found deliverance in imbibing the oppressors' ways of seeing the world, in telling the dvija's story through the dvija's gaze. Valmiki's protagonists freely shame and kill the low-born characters in the epic. Be it Shambhuka, the Shudra ascetic, who is killed by Lord Ram for performing tapascharya, or penance, that Shudras were forbidden to perform; or Surpankha, whose is cut off for confessing love to an Aryan prince. The unbearable irony of Valmiki's storytelling is captured in a poem by the famous poet Sachchidanand Hiranand Agyeya, 'Jo Pul Banayenge' (The Ones Who Built Bridges):

Senaye ho jayengee par
Maare jayenge Ravan
jayee honge Ram
jo nirmata rahe
itihaas mein
bandar kahalaye.

The armies shall cross

Ravan will be killed
Ram will be victorious
The builders/labourers
In history
Will be known as monkeys.

The poem is about the builders of the setu, the bridge, that took Ram and his army across the ocean to Lanka. The setu builders assisted in Ram's dharmayuddha against the immoral Ravana. They did all the labour but Valmiki wrote them into the story as monkeys. What mattered in the story was Ram's victory not who or what made it possible. The merit lay in victory not in building the bridge. The people who made possible Ram's victory were anointed as primates and non-humans. Valmiki depicted the monkeys as beholden because they had got a chance to serve the Lord.

Even the egalitarianism of the Bhakti ideology never translated into a lived reality. In fact, the social philosophy of the 'untouchable' Bhakti saints for all its radicalism actually worked subtly to keep caste hierarchies in place. The idea that the Bhakti movement was a radical and liberative force in Indian history was a post-Independence construct of nationalist poets and writers to demonstrate the deep, indigenous roots of Indian democracy. In reality, what appeared to be a radically egalitarian ideology was not all that egalitarian to begin with. An instance is the biographical narrative of Tiruppan Alvar, the Bhakti saint from the eight-ninth century who lived in a town near Srirangam Temple. Tiruppan used to sing praises to Lord Vishnu (as Ranganatha) but could not enter the temple because of his untouchable status. Lord Vishnu, pleased with the intensity of Tiruppan's devotion, appeared in the dream of the temple priest and urged him to bring Tiruppan to him. Tirrupan entered the temple, sang praises to the Lord and merged into the divine. But here was the catch to the story. Tiruppan entered the temple not on his feet but riding on the back of the temple priest. It was a radical proposition for an untouchable to have entered a temple but the story ensured that the temple itself was not sullied by Tiruppan's touch. His devotion brought him salvation but did not neutralize caste hierarchies. It continued to uphold Brahmanism as a spiritual ideal. Not social liberation but ideological mystification was doled out to the oppressed.

As a historian of the British empire and modern India, I had never cared for studying myths. To my mind, it was something the religious studies or ancient history folks did. I did real history, an empirical science that rested on objective and verifiable evidence. It wasn't for nothing that history was called a social science. It had its roots in the European Enlightenment, a philosophical movement in seventeenth and eighteenth century Europe identified with the Age of Reason. The institutionalization and professionalization of history as a discipline followed in the nineteenth century. history as it was practised in the university came to be conceived of as a rigorous science based on evidence. Since that time, notwithstanding the intellectual and ideological orientation of a historian, historical enquiry has been premised on the gathering and interpretation of evidence.

Over the years, however, my confidence in my discipline's explanatory potential began to fracture as I realized how our analytical frames, its categories, and its theories were so firmly tied to the ones generated in Europe. How did one make sense of pasts and human experiences that did not fit into those frames? Moreover, in some ways all history we wrote was attempting to show how we came to be, and where the present was a culmination of the past. However, what about pasts that did not flow into the present? Or how does one write about the past in the absence of evidence?

Coming out of the communal carnage of Partition, the historians of independent India had been firmly tied to notions of doing 'secular' and 'scientific' history. The rise of the Hindu right in the 1990s, and the shift in the world order with the fall of the Soviet Union in 1989, precipitated the need to re-examine the bearings of the discipline of history. The limitations of a historian's methodological repertoire were brought into relief in this battle of wits with a foe wielding the sword of the 'popular'—a popular which is not a 'massified, homogeneous structure' but one which has people as active agents, transforming, interpreting, rejecting, distinguishing, and classifying the world as they understood it. The historians faced with the might of the popular invoked reason, the objective language of truth, and the value of facts but to little avail. For it was quite possible that people could simultaneously read and believe in academic and popular conceptions of the past. After all the past and history were never the same but could always cohabit in our minds.

Thus the questions that confronted historians were:

What was the relation of the popular to the 'present'? Did the history we wrote have any relevance in the present? What was the relationship of history to the popular? What I gathered from these questions was that historians were being asked to revisit their relationship with time and the different modes of temporalization. That is, the ways that different people and communities adopt to deal with their past and their present; where the past and the present may not always be monochrome but ridden with dichotomies, non-homogenous characteristics and also may not be flowing continuously from one to the other. And where the 'historic' may not be part of the chronological past but a mythical present residing in the womb of memory. It is with these thoughts I had entered the world of Barbareek's myth.

Barbareek's myth was startling as it raised more questions than it answered. If myths nurtured and affirmed a society's sense of being, how was one to reconcile the apparent violence of the myths and the notion that India was a land of spirituality, tolerance, and non-violence? If myths legitimate social institutions and practices then why would there be such savagery in the myths especially if Hinduism was a way of life that believed in vasudhaiva kutumbakam, the world is one family? If myths assist in the creation of and in the maintenance of social cohesion, why would India's diversity which is a testament to Hinduism's tolerance be decimated in the myth? If myths anchor our present in the past, in which past was the notion that India was a land of non-violence anchored? Clearly the world of myths and what one knew of India wasn't adding up. I wondered if our myths played a very important role that had hitherto been hidden. A role of normalizing and invisibilizing violence in its various forms—pejorative naming, erasure of personhood, disembodying Barbareek, robbing Eklavya's thumb, asking Karna for his kavach-kundal, all done in the name of maintaining the order of things. This was blood justice. Our gods kill only to raise the Other to the divine status. Violence inflicted by the gods doesn't remain violence but becomes a narrative of redemption and liberation. Even violent battles and lynchings become dharmayuddha. Shrouded and concealed in religious myths, this was India's secret history of blood justice.

6

THE NON-ARYAN UTOPIA

Barbareek's myth made me wonder if there was a world of non-Aryan utopia(s) out there. Was there a universalism that held all the non-Aryan imaginations together? Or, like Valmiki, did the Dhangars, Khatiks, Chamars, Nats, and Banjaras all get subsumed into the Aryan utopia? If no, which traditions did they draw on? Which golden age did they imagine and subscribe to? How did they view 'Indian civilization'? As I pondered these questions, I was taken back to the earlier question of the relationship between history and the popular, the idea of time and the manner in which people experience it. To possess 'historical time' or to have a history indicated that one had some degree of social privilege. Having access to knowledge meant having access to power—the power to exist, power to be, power to choose, and the power to have a past. Writing history was an act of conferring existential legitimacy to individuals, peoples, and communities. The one who made it to history acquired the right to exist and thus became immortal. The people who remained outside became invisibilized, the 'people without history'. To arrive at their utopias, to have access to their worlds one had to step out of the confines of the world constituted by history textbooks.

It was an invitation to step into a world that history had, as luck would have it, failed to colonize.

The foray into the world of non-Aryan mythology brought home the story of King Bali, the mighty King of the Asuras, the demons. His tale embodied the non-Aryan utopia. His reign was believed to be a golden age. Bali was the grandson of Prahlad, also known as Bhakt Prahlad, the son of a Daitya or demon king, Hiranyakashipu. This is the same Prahlad whose story is usually told to children on chhoti Holi, when they go and worship the bonfire at a chowk wearing garlands made with biscuits, toffees, and dry fruits. Prahlad's father wanted to kill him for being a devotee of Vishnu. Hiranyakashipu made his sister, Holika, who was said to be immune to fire, sit in a burning pyre with Prahlad in her lap. However, it was Holika and not Prahlad who got burnt and Hiranyakashipu was eventually killed by the Narasimha (half-lion half-man) avatar. Prahlad's son was Virochana and his son was Bali. Like all tales there are different versions of the story of King Bali. One finds it in the Mahabharata, Ramayana, *Harivamsa, Bhavishya Purana, Brahma Purana, Brahamand Purana, Kurma Purana, Matsya Purana, Skanda Purana, Padma Purana, Vishnu Purana, Vamana Purana*, and *Vishnudharmottara Purana*.

The story goes that King Bali, despite being an Asura, was virtuous, restrained, and charitable. He once defeated Indra, the Lord of the Devtas, in a battle and subjugated the Trailokya, the three worlds. His reign over the three worlds was known as Satya Yuga, the Golden Age. He was described as a great ruler, a world guardian, a sacrificer, and giver of great gifts. Even Lakshmi, the goddess of wealth, having the radiance of a lotus petal, came with a lotus flower. She said to him: 'Since you have conquered the divine state by virtue of the valour you showed in the battlefield, I have, therefore, come to see you.' The celestial nymphs also came to serve Bali. However, Indra was unhappy with having lost his kingdom. He along with the other gods approached Brahma, the creator, and beseeched him to avenge his debacle.

King Bali in the meantime organized a sacrifice, the completion of which would have made him equal to Indra. At the start of the sacrifice, Bali declared that no one who attended the ceremony would be refused a boon. As the day progressed, a Vaman (a person of short stature) with matted hair, a stick, an umbrella, and a kamadala (a water pot) arrived at the sacrifice and began reciting the Vedas. King Bali was extremely pleased and offered him a boon. Bali's guru, Shukracharya, felt that there was something fishy and asked Bali to restrain himself. Bali, however, demurred. He firmly stated that he had offered the Vaman a boon and he would not take back his word. He once again asked the Vaman what he desired. The Vaman asked for a simple boon. Give me as much land as I can cover in three steps. The moment Bali agreed, the Vaman transformed himself into a giant. Just like Krishna he acquired the virat roop. With one enormous step he covered the entire Bhuloka, this world; with the second, the Bhuvarloka, the world of the departed; and with the third, Svarloka, the heavens. With three steps he covered the cosmos and took Bali's entire kingdom. Bali now had no place to go but to retreat to Pataal, the underworld.

The Vaman was actually an incarnation of Vishnu (and the son of sage Kashyap and his wife, Aditi) and had come to avenge Indra. He took the land from Bali and gave it to Indra who was pleased to have it back. In another version, Bali knew that the Vaman was an avatar of Vishnu even before he asked for the boon. He was so pleased to be visited and asked for a boon by Vishnu that he was willing to grant it, whatever it may be. The Vaman asked for land that could be covered in two-and-a-half steps. With two steps he covered the three worlds and had nowhere to place the remaining half step. King Bali being a man of his word asked the Vaman to place his foot on his head or his back. The Vaman did so and pushed Bali into the netherworld.

Why did the Vaman condemn and exile King Bali to Pataal? Why did he trick Bali into giving up his land? Bali's crime was that he had transgressed the order of things. He had violated the Asura's dharma. First, an Asura was supposed to remain in the netherworld. To know his place and not venture out from it. Bali's first transgression was that he ventured beyond the netherworld and captured the three realms and then tried to upstage Indra by performing the sacrifice. Secondly, an Asura was expected to be 'adharmic', that is, he was supposed to be disruptive, wily, and perform misdeeds of all kinds. His swadharma was not to follow dharma (his righteous conduct was to be unrighteous).

Bali transgressed his swadharma by being a righteous king. The *Vamana Purana* describes his reign thus: 'The entire world stood still in nature and began compliance of religion. As evils ceased, the spiritual conscience took root undeviated.' This was Bali's splendour but also his transgression. He had not only gone beyond his swadharma but also made 'time' come to a standstill. He had interrupted the unceasing dynamic of the world and thus disrupted the order of things. His punishment was that he was sent back to the netherworld restoring the order of things. And here is the twist in the story. While Indra was pleased to get his lands back, he was also impressed with Bali's large-hearted generosity and granted the lord of the Asuras a boon. Bali would wear the title of Indra in the future to come as a reward for his generosity. The way Barbareek bore the title of Krishna.

This mythical story of Bali has resonated with many people. One of them was Jyotiba Phule. He was born in 1827 in a village in Satara district, Maharashtra. Phule couldn't make sense of Bali's exile. Why would a man's generosity be used against him? What was the meaning of King Bali's land being taken away? In raising these questions, Phule was lifting the iron weight of several generations of tradition and mental servitude. If there was anything that the tradition forbade, it was to ask a question. This tradition after all had come down to us through the great sages and was the repository of Indian civilization. All was lost if you questioned it. Nevertheless, Phule persisted. Too irreverent a man to stop at just asking this question. He mocked the tradition, lampooned it, and jeered at it. He was an iconoclast who tore down the entire edifice of Vedic learning. His pen ripped into the epistemic dominance of ancient texts by turning it on its head. The Vedas for him were nothing more than Brahmanical mythology.

In all myths, the low-born characters, from Bali to Barbareek to Eklavya and Karna, are presented as generous to the extent that none of them cry foul at being robbed of their life. In fact they willingly give it away. What does their lack of protest say? What kind of consciousness does it reflect? For Phule the answer was simple: the essence of Indian civilization was not tolerance but violence. The profound religious conservatism of his people kept their consciousness enslaved. The only way to smash this consciousness was to break the hold of ritualistic religion which positioned the Brahmins at the top of the hierarchy. Phule's writings were not meant for the educated urban middle classes or the intelligentsia. Neither was he writing to acquire social mobility nor to get invitations to polite dinner parties or for foreign lecture tours. He was writing to explode the Brahmanical bogey and to awaken his people who were landless peasants and menial workers. Phule was forging a new political identity through his writings.

Jyotiba Phule appears alongside Raja Ram Mohan Roy, Keshub Chandra Sen, Henry Vivian Derozio, Dayanand Saraswati, Vivekananda, and Gandhi as makers of modern India in school textbooks and university courses. However, he was unlike the others. His birth status as a Shudra of the Mali (gardener) caste did not ensure an easy access to reading and writing. He was born in a world where access to the written word was a privilege not a right. Even if one learnt to read and write, it was difficult to find avenues to express oneself in the high languages—Sanskrit, English or Persian. The act of writing has for long been used in history to colonize, to dominate, to oppress, to outlaw tongues, and to silence speech. Writing as a mode of aesthetic self-expression has consequently eluded the subaltern for the longest time in history resulting in the literary erasure of their lives and experiences. It was the educational institutions set up by the Christian missionaries in the nineteenth century that opened up new avenues of learning and advancement for the lower-caste communities. Phule received education at one such mission school. The peers and the literature he encountered at the different educational institutions that he attended were seminal in Phule's formation. Quite early on, he was exposed to Christian missionary propaganda, Orientalist texts (H. H. Wilson, R. E. Enthoven, Captain Cook's voyages, Max Müeller, John Wilson, and the Bible), the writings of European religious radicals such as Thomas Paine and Martin Luther, and the Hindu reformers.

For Phule, writing was about empowerment, self-reclamation, defiance, and self-assertion. His writings (a play, ballads, short books, speeches, lectures, and statements) embodied a new moral imagination, harboured alternate realities and thereby presented a sharp political critique of the context in which they were produced. Phule employed a rustic Marathi dialectic with colloquialisms to reach out to his community and, at the same time, used the language of the colonial masters to write memorandums and statements. He wrote short books that were priced cheaply so the poor could buy them. The indelible imprint they left on the world was not an unintended consequence but one prefigured in the act of writing itself. He meant his books to irk, enrage, and outrage the powers that be. His writings remind one of the bestselling 'forbidden' literature (the salacious, blasphemous, and treasonous literary underground) in eighteenth century France that desacralized the royalty and eventually contributed to the fall of the ancien régime.

Jyotiba Phule's book *Gulamgiri* (Slavery) written in 1873 sought to free his people from a consciousness that kept them enslaved. He did so by turning the idea of the superiority of the Aryan race on its head. The narrative of the book is a conversation between two literary characters Dhondirao and Jotirao. He begins by dismantling the origin story of the caste system as it appears in Purusha Sukta, a hymn from the tenth mandala of the Rig Veda, dedicated to the Purusha, the 'cosmic being'. (The Brahmans were born out of the mouth of Brahma, the Kshatriyas out of the shoulders, the Vaishyas out of the thighs and the Shudras out of the feet.) He attacked it by inverting the dashavatara story (the story of the ten avatars of Vishnu) and presenting each of the avatars as Aryan invaders from Iran. In Phule's reconstruction, the sixth avatar is Brahma and he is credited with giving birth to the caste system. Phule 'empiricized' the myth. That is, he took it at face value and mocked it for its absurdity. Dhondirao wonders how Brahma was able to give birth from different parts of his body. He wondered: if indeed he gave birth to four castes then shouldn't he have had eight breasts, four belly buttons, four vaginas, and four anuses. 'Yadi sachmuch mein Brahma ko chaar muha hote to usi hisaab se use aath stan, chaar nabhiyan, chaar yoniyan aur chaar maldwaar hone chahiye.' Jotirao expressed astonishment at who took care of

Brahma's household work with all four vaginas menstruating for nearly sixteen days of the month. 'In chaar angon ki yoni, maahwaar (rajaswala) ke karan, uski kul milakar solah din ke liye ashuddh ho kar door-door rahna pada hoga. Phir sawal uthta hai ki uske ghar ka kaam-dhanda kaun karta hoga?' The irreverent tone continues throughout the text. It goes to the extent of condemning Brahma for all manner of sins; it was the reason why no one worshipped him. In another text, Phule denounced the story of Brahma as the progenitor of castes by using Darwin's evolutionary theory. This was an anti-myth of what Phule called the myth of Aryan superiority. It placed the dvija (Brahmin, Kshatriya, and Vaishya) in the category of Aryans and the Shudra, untouchables, tribals, and Muslims in the non-Aryan category.

After breaking down the origin myth, Jotirao pitched the kingdom of Bali as the golden age, not just as the one that existed in the past but one that embodied the utopic future. This was not the Ram Rajya of Gandhi or the Hindu Rashtra of Savarkar but the Sata Yuga, the Age of Truth, of Bali's reign. This utopia was a casteless and just society reminiscent of Sant Ravidas's 'Begumpura', a city without sorrow. In Phule's writing, King Bali replaced Ram and Krishna as the purushottam, ideal human and king. The name Bali means possessor of strength, the power one needed to cultivate the land and fight for it. The word bali also means the 'sacrificial offering' or the 'blood victim'. King Bali embodied both meanings of the word. Phule narrates the story of the Vaman avatar robbing Bali of his kingdom. He consistently used a colloquial term of abuse to address the Vaman. Traditionally the stories of King Bali as a just king were already popular. In drawing on Bali, Phule was projecting his own interpretation on to the pre-existing cultural and social consciousness of the lower castes ensuring that his message fell on receptive soil. It was the familiar story imbued with new meaning. Phule at times conflated the imagery of Bali with that of Shivaji. Especially in a ballad that he wrote in 1869. Both imageries appealed to Phule's cultivator-warrior community.

Rescuing the lower castes from the clutches of superstition was only part of Phule's concerns. The other was to draw attention to the present-day conditions of the Shudra community. In one text, Phule lists the different kinds of labour that the Shudras performed. They looked after and fed the animals; cleaned up the cattle dung and lifted it on their heads; tilled the land; tended the crops; looked after the horses in the homes of the Brahmins; cleaned their homes; did their dishes; daubed and painted their houses with dung; worked as coolies in railway and bus stations; collected trash and sold waste; bathed the upper-caste people and dressed them. In return, the Brahmins ensured that Shudras didn't learn to read and write; were barred from rituals; portrayed as lazy; and treated as untouchables. In the context of British rule, what made it worse was that the Brahmin's traditional privilege now extended to the non-religious realm as well. Brahmins occupied the majority of government/bureaucratic positions (schoolmasters, clerks, education officers etc.) and were using them to protect their caste interests. The few Shudras who did manage to get a school education had very few job openings and were still stuck servicing the elite. Phule emphatically reiterated this point in all his writings. He redefined the term Shudra in his writings. Shudra not just referred to a ritually impure caste but an oppressed community and one that also included the untouchables (Shudra, Ati Shudra, Kunbi, Mali, Mang, and Mahar). Phule was thus the first to talk of the problems facing India's village economy, the landless labourers, and the urban poor.

He also identified the fact that patriarchy and the oppression of lower castes went hand in hand. For him inequality within the family (the low position of women) was akin to caste oppression. Educating his wife, Savitribai, was Phule's way of rejecting both patriarchy and casteism. They eventually started a school for Dalit and Muslim girls in Pune in August 1848. This incurred the wrath of Phule's family and community. Driven out of their neighbourhood, the Phules moved to a Dalit working class area in Pune and restarted the school there. This school was an unrivalled pedagogical experiment. They focused on giving the girl students vocational training so that they could become self-reliant. Disinterest in education and a high dropout rate plagued the community. The syllabus was thus geared to the interests of Dalit children to prevent them from dropping out. They started literacy and awareness campaigns amongst the parents to sensitize them to the importance of education. The students in no time began to shine. A fourteen-year student wrote a prize-winning essay that talked about her life as a Shudra:

The people who dress themselves up and parade around in their purity have only one intention, and that is to think that they are more pure than other people, and they feel happy at this; but do their cruel hearts ever feel any pity at the suffering that we endure that the very touch of our hands pollutes them?

The 'long and ferocious' essay was the fruit of Phule and Savitribai's labour.

In 1873, two years before Dayanand Saraswati established the Arya Samaj, Phule founded the Satyashodhak Samaj, the truth-seeking society, in Pune. The samaj started by arranging marriages without priests and dowry. The main work of the samaj was to create awareness in the low-caste communities about the oppression that they faced, enable them to get an education, and encourage them to be more articulate in the public sphere in order to enhance their visibility. The Satyashodhak Samaj created a groundswell of change fed by Phule's anti-feudal stance and peasant agrarian distress. The samaj was to later inspire several similar movements in different parts of India. These were the Ad Dharm movement in Punjab (constituted of young educated Chamars who broke away from the Arya Samaj), the Adi Hindu movement of Swami Achutanand in Uttar Pradesh in the 1920s, Adi Andhra, Adi Dravid, and Adi Karnataka in southern India. An important variable in their mobilization was the economic distress in the wake of World War I and the introduction of the Montagu-Chelmsford Reforms in 1919. These movements challenged and reversed the view that the Aryans were the original inhabitants of the subcontinent and the makers of Indian civilization. They vigorously took up the issue of lower castes' access to communal water tanks and to the temples and also encouraged their people to stop performing the traditional caste duties.

Phule thus laid the foundations of an alternate discourse in the Indian subcontinent that led to the rise of leaders such as Iyothee Thass, Maraimalai Adigal, Periyar, and Ambedkar in the 1930s and 1940s, who took the cause of the 'depressed classes' or Dalits up to a wider regional and national level. In the post-Independence era a strong Dalit literary movement developed. Writing which had been the preserve of the upper caste and elites now was being made use of by individuals from the suppressed and subordinate groups. They wrote in the languages and dialects they knew. Writers such as Daya Pawar, Namdeo Dhasal, Baburao Bagul, Keshav Meshram, Narayan Surve, Raja Dhale, Gangadhar Pantawane, Vaman Nimbalkar, and Omprakash Valmiki waged a valiant battle against caste oppression by writing about their lives and the discrimination they had faced. Protest and testimony were central aspects of their writings. The injustice done to the mythical Bali had played its part in catalysing a long-lasting rebellion against the tyranny of religion and caste privilege. The seeds of Phule, the gardener, were flowering.

Despite the blooms, why did the Indian garden remain a wasteland when it came to Phule's ideology taking root? This was a question that kept nettling me. Why was it that notwithstanding the substantial gains of lower-caste assertion, it was the myth of Aryan superiority that eventually thrived as national ideology? How did the notion that Sanskrit possessed an all-India character and constituted the 'high tradition', despite evidence to contrary, become popular? Why did the non-Sanskrit and the non-Aryan tradition come to be seen as the 'low tradition' and thereby lose visibility in the 'mainstream' public sphere? Perhaps the answers lay in the radical nature of lower-caste mobilization and its consequent separation from the wider networks of nationalist mobilization; and the hijacking of their symbols and constituency by upper-caste movements. These issues were apparent from Phule's time onwards. For instance, Phule's appeal to the British to pass legislation to protect the interests of the lower castes did not bear much fruit because his agenda of social reorganization challenged the colonial state's alignment with the Indian English-educated elite. The British could not abandon the very premise of the structure they had created in favour of carrying out reforms as envisioned by Phule. Even Satyashodhak Sabha's mobilization got hijacked with Bal Gangadhar Tilak starting the Ganpati Festival in 1898 and Shivaji's co-option as the gobrahman pratipalak—a Brahmin and an anti-Muslim Leader. With time the Satyashodhak followers who belonged to the non-Brahmin middle castes began to use the word Kshatriya (used by Phule at times to denote the original inhabitants who were oppressed by Aryans) and as being of Aryan descent and reserved the term non-Aryan (or Shudra) for untouchables and tribals. Hereafter, such loss of symbols and constituency to the larger nationalist mobilization remained a recurrent and intractable problem.

With the Gandhian mobilization a greater number of non-Brahmins began to get drawn into the Indian National Congress. Although the Congress drained the lower-caste movements of its members, it failed to address the issue of caste oppression in any substantial manner. Similar was the problem with the left movement which remained focused on the issues of the urban proletariat. It did not focus on the caste question for fear of splintering the movement. The ambivalent relationship between the Communists and the Dalits was reflected in B. R. Ambedkar's opposition to the Communist-led mill strike in 1929 in Bombay. He argued that the strike imposed hardships on the economically and socially weaker lower-caste groups as had happened during the strike in 1928. He felt that the trade union leadership had failed to take up the issue specific to lower-caste mill workers, such as, their being debarred from employment in the higher-paying weaving departments of the mills. The Dalit movement, as a result, developed in isolation. It had significant but limited political gains (and many remained unrealized until the making of the Indian Constitution). Furthermore, until B. R. Ambedkar and Periyar became politically active, the nationalist arena didn't have publicly visible and educated lower-caste spokesmen despite significant mobilization. When one did receive an education one was either co-opted by the elite or one yielded to the class status that one acquired with education and one's professional location; or one simply sought to hide one's caste and to pass as socially acceptable. So while strong social critiques and viewpoints existed, they did not acquire influence or dominance in the public sphere.

Ambedkar also remained ambivalent about taking up only the cause of the lower caste and untouchables in the 1920s. It is only in the 1930s that he responded to the groundswell of change and came all out to fight for the Dalit cause.

In post-Independence school textbooks Jyotiba Phule was co-opted as a maker of modern India but his ideas were set aside. It is ironic how the early reformers from Raja Ram Mohan Roy to the nationalists generated anti-Brahmanical ideas and critiques but their philosophies promoted the Aryan myth; and how all these philosophies rendered the violence of caste system invisible and constructed the Muslim and the Christian as the Other. Through the passing decades the question of violence—physical, epistemic, symbolic, imagined—and its experience remained unaddressed. The psychology and the societal structure that produced violence also remained intact. The myths continued to be told and retold; the Khatu Shyamji Temple continued to draw multitudes of pilgrims year after year; Ganpati and Durga puja celebrations became more and more elaborate; Shivaji became Brahmin and Onam transformed into a festival to celebrate the Vaman avatar instead of King Bali. Violence was nurtured, sustained, and rendered invisible by our myths that came in different garbs. As a result of all this, no amount of constitutional provisions could nullify the myths of Aryan superiority and India being a land of non-violence.

7

THE HISTORICAL VICTIMS

While researching my grandfather's life in Indore, there was an incident that my uncle mentioned in passing that caught my interest. This was regarding a Hindu-Muslim riot that took place in Indore. His memory was fuzzy about the date. All he remembered was that it happened because of a dispute over a Muslim julusa, procession. I dived into the post-Independence history of Indore and found some scholarly works that mentioned a riot in the year 1989. If researching the history of the late-nineteenth century world had required wading through multiple forms of print culture, the 1980s were about moving images teleported into our homes and the new audio culture. Television with multiple private channels, the cable network, satellite TV, portable audio cassette players and video cassette recorders (VCR) and video compact discs (VCD) were revolutionizing the everyday lives of people and informing their sense of self. The tele-serialization of the stories of the Ramayana and Mahabharata, the flooding of the market with posters of Lord Ram wearing a crown and with his bow and quiver of arrows, and images of Bharat Mata holding a saffron flag were creating a new aesthetic sensibility. Communications technology would undergo other revolutions with the coming of the internet in the 1990s and social media, smartphones and handheld devices in the 2000s. Technology and communitarian propaganda were indeed merry bedfellows.

On the morning of 13 October 1989, the Muslim processionists carrying green flags on Milad un-Nabi to mark the birthday of the Prophet wound through the main avenues of Indore. As the procession reached the Ram Laxman Chowk area some crackers or, as some reports said, 'bombs' went off towards the back of the procession. The processionists were supposedly carrying weapons hidden in their bamboo staffs in anticipation of trouble. They confronted the policemen lined up on the streets for managing the procession. The altercation escalated and soon turned into a full-blown riot. The government had to issue a 'shoot at sight' order to quell the communal flames. Abdul Gaffoor Noori, a wealthy Muslim and the president of the Anjuman-Islahul-Muslimeen, an organization engaged in the interpretation of Islamic law, had planned the procession. He had political aspirations and wanted the procession to be a show of strength. Some local Muslim leaders including the shahar qazi, the chief religious head, were not as sanguine about organizing the procession but Noori, despite their opposition, had gone ahead with it.

This was not the first time a religious procession had turned into communal conflict. This was an old phenomenon since the anti-cow-killing agitations of 1890s—processions had served as important sites of religious conflict. A procession, with a congregation of believers marching together for a shared cause or for their beliefs, carries great symbolic value. Inviting broader participation, the processions serve as an integrative force and thereby nurture and foster a community identity. However, a procession also carries subversive potential because it traverses different kinds of residential, public, and sacred spaces that people of other communities perceive as theirs. This penetration or breach of territoriality by the procession is not always appreciated and becomes a cause of inter-community conflict.

Noori had decided to organize the procession in response to a massive Vishwa Hindu Parishad (VHP) rally that was held in Indore on 30 September 1989. A few days before the riot, members of various Hindu organizations had taken out a 'Ramshila Pujan' procession on 4 October. The processionists carried consecrated bricks for the construction of the Ram temple in Ayodhya. The VHP had launched the Ram Janmabhoomi movement in 1984. It sought to reclaim the Babri Masjid, a fifteenth-century mosque built by one of the generals of the invading army of Babur, purportedly on the site of Lord Ram's birth in Ayodhya. Here was the classic clash between the mythic world of Lord Ram's birth story and history as it happened. The Ram Janmabhoomi mobilization mimicked that of the erstwhile gaurakshini sabhas. The VHP was formed in 1964 on the day of Krishna Janmashtami by M. S. Golwalkar and S. S. Apte in Bombay in the presence of Sikh leaders and representatives of the Hindu community from Trinidad and Kenya. The ceremony was held at the centre of a Hindu missionary movement led by Swami Chinmayananda. They organized World Hindu conventions on the occasion of the Kumbh Mela in the city of Allahabad. It was a way of reaching out to thousands of laity who were coming to the festival. The organization drew on the traditional networks of communication to create a national community. The VHP leaders also focused their energy on mobilizing Hindus abroad and doing missionary work amongst untouchable tribal communities. Setting the VHP apart from other organizations was its distinctly modernist, inclusive, and nationalist tenor. It drew inspiration from Vivekananda's writings and the manner in which he had made Hinduism part of a global conversation.

The years preceding the riots in 1989 had seen a build-up of communal tensions in the city of Indore that had otherwise been relatively free of communal tensions since Independence. The anti-Sikh riots in 1984 that had followed Prime Minister Indira Gandhi's assassination and the agitation around the infamous Shah Bano Case in 1985 marked the turning points in the city's inter-communal history. Shah Bano was a resident of Indore and had gone to court seeking alimony from her divorced husband. The court had granted her relief but the Congress government, under pressure from Muslim clerics, reversed the judgment by an act of Parliament. Noori had spearheaded the agitation against the Supreme Court judgment pronouncing it as being against the Sharia. He is believed to have mobilized the clerics of different mosques into creating a groundswell of protest against the judgment. Noori insisted that it was the divorced woman's family and community that should look after her and promised to issue a fatwa forcing the husband to pay her alimony. Thereafter, Shah Bano changed her stance and asked for the withdrawal of the Supreme Court judgment. The legal dynamics apart, the Shah Bano case created acrimony between the Hindu and Muslim communities in Indore. An instance of this was a Hindu reporter in a press conference asking Z. A. Ansari, a Congress (I) worker and the state minister of environment at the time, if he would go off to Pakistan in the event the Supreme Court's judgment wasn't reversed. (Ansari was supporting the view taken by Noori and the chief mufti of Indore.)

The dynamics of electoral politics was the other variable impacting inter-community relations in the city at this time. The announcement of elections earlier in 1989 had sharpened the political jockeying in the state. The rival political groups had begun covertly courting different community leaders for their votes. The Ram Janmabhoomi movement mobilized various sections of society in favour of the Bharatiya Janata Party (BJP), a national party formed in 1980. It had morphed out of the Bharatiya Jan Sangh which was formed in 1951 by Syama Prasad Mookerjee and rose to strength on the back of the Ram Janmabhoomi movement. The BJP held special appeal for lower-caste Hindus as it provided them a platform to participate in a larger Hindu identity. In Indore, on the Hindu side, it was the Chamars, the leather workers and Sonkar Khatiks, the Hindu butchers specializing in pig meat, who were at the forefront of communal mobilization. In mixed, lower-income neighbourhoods, Hindu rioters specifically targeted Muslim houses. Muslim miscreants on the other hand targeted Hindu shops and a nursing home. Interestingly, a similar pattern of the involvement of the lower-caste Hindus, especially the Sonkar caste of pig farmers, pig butchers, and pig bristle manufacturers, was evident in the post-Babri Masjid demolition riots in Kanpur in 1992. The Sonkars, as specialists in handling pigs and their meat, resent the Muslims for the Islamic prohibition against pork consumption. Consequently, cow protection held a special appeal for them and also made them more open to accepting the Hindu identity. The Sonkars getting sucked into the VHP maelstrom was reminiscent of the co-option of the movement of the Balmikis, Jats, and women's empowerment groups by the Hindu right during the colonial period.

An interesting pattern in low-caste mobilization was discernible in this period. While the Khatiks in Kanpur were being empowered, the ones in Haryana were under threat of being lynched by a mob. A new avatar of the gauraksha movement arose on the sidelines of the Ram Janmabhoomi movement in places where the mobilization in the name of Lord Ram did not beget an emotive response. Here the image of the 'gau' became a rallying force. The state of Haryana was an example. Since the late nineteenth century, the Arya Samaj's gaurakhsha movement had made inroads in Haryana to the extent that gauraksha had become an integral part of the Jat identity. There were several popular ballads and folktales that valorized the Jat as a gaurakshak who saved the cow from the assault of the Muslim butcher. Several cities in Haryana were ravaged by anti-cow-killing riots in the 1920s. The VHP once again invoked gauraksha as a rallying cry to charm the Jats into a new and more modern assimilative Hindu identity. This new mobilization centred around the cow led to an increased number of public attacks and the killing of Muslims and Dalits.

The announcement of elections in October 1989 had been preceded and followed by a series of communal riots in north, central and western India, especially in states where the Congress (I), the ruling party, was in power. The leader of the Congress, Rajiv Gandhi, had announced early elections to combat the growing strength of the opposition led at the time by Vishwanath Pratap Singh. Rajiv had followed in the footsteps of his mother, Indira Gandhi, the president of the Congress (I), who had risen to power in the 1970s by appeasing the minorities and the weaker sections of the society. However, since the early 1980s, the Congress had tried to mobilize Hindu middle caste votes in its favour by gently fanning the activities of the VHP and exploiting the Meenakshipuram conversions of several low-caste Hindus to Islam in 1981. Rajiv Gandhi, as the prime minister, authorized the shilanyas, laying the foundation stone, for the Ram temple in Ayodhya in order to placate the VHP in 1986. So the vote game of the ruling party and the BJP-led Ram Janmabhoomi-Babri Masjid movement had polarized the electorate. Reports said that the Ramshila Pujan procession in Indore was conducted with the full knowledge of the then Home Minister, Buta Singh. At the time the Congress Party was in power in Madhya Pradesh and people used the opportunity to criticize the chief minister and the incompetence of the administration. The local police and the district administration were believed to have been complicit in letting the riot get out of hand.

Riots are never spontaneous. They serve a 'functional

role' in electoral politics by helping the perpetrators gain the support of their community. The cycles of flaring up of riots and their subsidence often follow the electoral cycles of Indian politics. The invocation of emotionally charged notions of self—Hindus as protectors of the cow and Muslims as conniving beef-eaters—continues to be the easiest way to set off rumours and to mobilize a mob especially when the area is gearing up for upcoming elections. Once community identities come to be seen as mutually antagonistic they become perfect constituencies for mobilization from above by politicians who make use of these identities based on their political and material calculations or by religious leaders who do faith-based politics. Thus, the identity of Hindus and Muslims forged in the crucible of conflict became an easy tool in electoral politics. However, the numbers and frequency of the riots in the 1980s was something India had not seen since its Partition in 1947.

The violence that occurred during Partition had played a significant role in furthering the notion that Hindus and Muslims were two separate, antagonistic communities. Thereafter, the idea found its way into everyday life, as well as literature, cinema, and the arts and thereby seeped into the popular psyche. Several post-independence writers and litterateurs such as Amrita Pritam, Agyeya, Saadat Hasan Manto, Bapsi Sidhwa, Khushwant Singh, Mumtaz Mufti, Naseem Hijazi, and Krishna Baldev Vaid to name a few, captured the communal frenzy at the time of Partition in their works. *Tamas* (Darkness), a novel written in 1974 by Bhisham Sahni, the secretary of Progressive Writers' Association and a member of the Indian Peoples' Theatre Association, is one such novel. In the story, a Muslim politician commissions a Dalit to slaughter a pig. The next morning the pig's carcass is found on the footsteps of a mosque. The enraged Muslims retaliate by killing a cow and throwing it in front of a temple, eventually leading to bloodshed between the Hindu and Muslim communities. Sahni further shows how the riot was linked to and made use of by politicians to get tickets to fight the upcoming local elections. The novel is replete with imageries of sectarian violence: an adolescent young man stabs an elderly Muslim to death; Vanaprasthi, a Hindu holy man, incites young men to carry out violence; a gang of young Muslim men forces a Sikh to convert and circumcise him, Iqbal Singh becomes Iqbal Ahmad; a Muslim mob sets the Hindu-owned grain-market on fire; and a Hindu woman is gang-raped by Muslim men. The novel, while written from a 'secular' perspective nevertheless reproduces much of the standard imagery that the gaurakshini movement had deployed in the early twentieth century: the wily Muslim politician, Muslims as rapists, and the Muslims' desire for conversion.

◆

Haroon, a lower-caste Muslim of the metalworkers community (Lohars), was one of the people who suffered losses in the riot of 1989 in Indore. The rioters had claimed the lives of several innocent people. There were reports of attacks on some Hindu businesses, and arson and looting in low-income Muslim mohallas, neighbourhoods. Most Muslims in

Indore were educationally and economically backward. Post-independence industrialization and economic development had either been ruinous for them or had marginalized them. Some Muslims had done well because of their earnings from Gulf countries where they would go for a few years to work as labourers. The bulk of the people affected by the violence came from the lower-caste groups of the Muslims (such as Chipas, Lohars, or Julahas). While Haroon's family was safe, Haroon's godown, where he stored metal chairs, was gutted. Haroon's father was amongst the few who had done well and bought himself a shop next to my grandfather's in the Loha Bazaar. Haroon was nearly the same age as one of my uncles. My grandfather trusted Haroon and would leave him in charge of his shop whenever he had to go out. After his godown was burnt down, my grandfather repaired Haroon's chairs in his factory and helped him get credit by acting as his guarantor. There were numerous such stories of people from either community bringing people into their homes or coming to their rescue in different ways. On a recent visit to Indore, we drove through the Loha Mandi and to my utter surprise I saw that Haroon kaka's store had a board named 'Vishal Steel Products' hanging on it. I asked my cousin, who was driving the car, about the store. He confirmed that it was indeed Haroon kaka's store but he had changed the name to a 'Hindu' one after some riot. I instantly knew which riot it was.

The fact that my grandfather extended support to Haroon was in keeping with what I knew of him. He was a patriarch, who was hard-working, generous, honest, and just. There was a constant stream of aunts, uncles, relatives, and friends passing through the household in Indore at all hours of the day. I distinctly remember that we always had either some ageing relative or a friend of my grandfather's who had been turned away by their family living with us. My grandfather was an irreverent man and did not observe most of the purifying rituals of a dvija household. Much to my grandmother's annoyance he wouldn't bathe until midday. It fell to my grandmother to enforce order. I could always hear her cursing her daughters-in-law and shouting at my unmarried aunts and uncles to bathe before they ate in the morning, to keep shoes out of the kitchen, not to put one's hand into the earthen water pot to draw out water, and threatening menstruating female relatives not to touch the achaar ki barni, the pickle container. In the summers when we would visit him he would bring us a sack of ripe mangoes and leave them soaked in water. We would strip down to our chemises and squat around a big bowl for a feast of cool mangoes. He was also a willing playmate when he visited our Delhi home. He got me my first piggy-bank, shaped like a squirrel, and taught me to play chess.

For once, however, I was finding it difficult to separate the person my grandfather was with the ideology that he espoused. For him the ideology of the VHP (and earlier of the Jan Sangh) was an extension of his belief in the Arya Samaj. Several questions raced through my mind. What kept him from cheering Haroon's loss or wishing a sword had run through him? They were friendly but not really friends. They never visited each other on Diwali or Eid. But then again, does espousing a supremacist ideology necessarily fill people with unremitting hatred towards the Other? Or was my grandfather's generosity an example of the proverbial market-place cordiality that Adam Smith and Montesquieu so emphatically upheld in their writings? The market sublimating people's manners and ways of thinking. I wondered if there was a direct causal connection between one's ideology and one's everyday life. Or did they both function on a different axis? Maybe he was following Apad Dharma, in which one suspends ideology in an extreme situation? Maybe they experienced the riot as one experiences a natural calamity where everyone is believed to be equally affected and therefore deserving of sympathy. I tried to evaluate the incident from various angles.

Perhaps Haroon had my grandfather's sympathy as the incident had affected him and had nothing to do with killing a cow or it wasn't a question of a female relative wanting to marry a low-caste Muslim? My thoughts circled back to earlier questions about the relationship between ideology and personal actions. So, although my family did not go out and participate in violence, were they still accountable? Wasn't the historical and logical culmination of their ideology a riot such as this one? I struggled with these questions as I sat at the dining table that morning making paper flowers for my son's school's craft activity. My mind turned the different corners of the maze and walked into walls as my eyes traced the movement of the scissors. I was having a hard time shaping the petals as the hands of the clock moved briskly towards the arrival of the school bus. I was constantly aware of the thoughts that whirled through my mind that the connections

I was making between history, ideology and human action didn't necessarily match with my grandfather's response to Haroon. I was the one holding court, playing counsel, and passing the verdict. Impugning them one moment and absolving them the next.

This episode actually had a completely different meaning in his world. In his view, he had done a genuine favour to Haroon by being his guarantor. It reflected his large-heartedness. This was regardless of the fact that Muslims were given to violence, 'Mussalman hinsak pravitti ke log hote hain.' Violence was what the Muslims were prone to doing to satisfy their lust for meat and women. Muslims were violent, not us. We were Vaishnavas. Vaishnavism had such a long and deep connection with ahimsa. Vaishnavas did not even hurt animals, let alone humans. A Hindu sees God in every particle and worships truth, non-violence, and peace. There was not even a sliver of violence in our identity. Even our food habits differentiated us from the Mussalmans. We never ate from the same communal plate as the Muslims did; we never ate bread, biscuits, cakes or bakery products, not even on birthdays; our food was saatvik while that of the Muslims was tamasik; after all, jaisa ann vaisa mann, one's sensibilities were determined by one's food. The Muslims were born with sharper canine teeth that helped them tear meat. The Quran said that kafirs, non-believers, should be killed and slaughtered. They were promised jannat ki hoorain, celestial nymphs, if they died fighting for Islam.

In helping Haroon, my grandfather was not making an exception because it was in line with his dharma. However, this did not take away from what he believed of Muslims. Muslims had always victimized Hindus right from Ghazni's invasions—the destruction of the idol and the slaughter of ten thousand Brahmins praying inside the Somnath Temple; Ghazni repeatedly looted Somnath; the desecration of the birthplaces of Ram, Krishna, and Shiva and the building of mosques over them; the destruction of five lakh Hindu temples; the oppression that Hindus had suffered under Mughal rule; the abuse and rape of innumerable Hindu mothers, daughters, and sisters; the imposition of jaziya on unsuspecting Hindu traders; the jauhar of Rajput women to save themselves from randy Muslims; the Hindu wives that the Mughals took; the killing of thousands of sadhus, sants, and cows; the wily Muslims' attempts to convert by slyly feeding you beef; their partitioning of our country in 1947; the killing and driving into exile of lakhs of Hindu Pandits in Kashmir. There were thirty million Muslims in India at the time of Independence and by 2002 there were 350 million; there are 35,000 slaughterhouses in India where 50,000 cattle are being slaughtered every day; the Muslims never sing Vande Mataram, the national song. In this worldview, the instances of Hindu persecution and Muslim crimes really did stack up. At the same time, the fact that it was the Muslims and lower-caste Hindus who were involved in violence helped my family distance themselves from it. After all they were reading about the riots in newspapers or learning about it through the news on TV while sipping their tea.

◆

A discourse is an organized expression of ideas and thoughts; and often, like our myths, it has little or no grounding in reality. It is just a set of words that circulate across time and space. Nevertheless, a discourse that surrounds people often becomes the filter through which they experience and engage with the world; and the way they experience the world reinforces their pre-existing belief systems. Discourse and experience together become interpenetrating layers of consciousness, each feeding off the other. Citing historical evidence to refute the notion of 'Hindu persecution' would have been futile because this discourse is independent of facts, historical or otherwise. It harbours its own truths. It is premised on belief. Saying that the number of Muslims killed in post-Independence riots was more than that of Hindus and that it was Haroon who was the victim because it was his godown that was burnt down was therefore irrelevant. My grandfather's community was still the victim or, as they say, the 'victimized non-victims'. Then there was the example of Bharmall. He had not killed the Muslim butcher but had self-immolated. The Muslim butcher had not stopped despite Bharmall's pleas. Bharmall, the dharmaraj, was not an aggressor but a historical victim. He had raised a hand only to beseech the aggressor to stop. This is the discourse of Hindu victimhood that many of us grow up with. It seeps into our consciousness unseen like water soaking cotton wool. The presence is invisible but a presence nevertheless.

A PARABLE OF OUR TIMES

In 1899, a young black sharecropper, on a farm outside Atlanta in the United States of America, got into a dispute with his landlord and ended up killing him in self-defence. A rumour circulated that he had raped the landlord's wife. A white mob of nearly 4,000 people collected to watch the anticipated lynching of the black sharecropper. W. E. B. Du Bois (1868–1963), an African-American with a PhD from Harvard, who taught sociology at Atlanta University, heard about the prospective lynching, prepared a letter of protest and rushed to deliver it to the local newspaper. But he was already too late. The white mob jeered and clapped as the black man, cowering in fear was caught, stripped, tortured and, in the end, hanged. On his way to the newspaper office, Du Bois learned that the black man had been 'barbecued'. That is, the victim was hanged and burnt alive at the stake, left to slowly simmer and get roasted. Du Bois also heard that the victim's knuckles were being exhibited as a souvenir at a nearby grocery store. This lynching changed the course of Du Bois's life and he went on to become a leading African-American civil rights activist. He is known for an evocative collection of essays, *The Souls of Black Folk* (1903). Described as 'fireworks going off in a cemetery', the book eventually became the Bible of the civil rights movement.

Do you know where the word 'lynch' comes from? It comes from America, the land of liberty. For long, the word 'lynch' was used as part of the system of frontier justice in America where the absence of legally-sanctioned trials and punishments justified its use. The verb 'lynch' could include whipping and capital punishment. However, it was only after the American Civil War (1861–65), and following the emancipation of slaves (1863), that it came to be firmly associated with 'to put to death' and became synonymous with acts of retribution reserved for the free African-Americans. The post-emancipation era saw the rise in racial discrimination and segregation—prejudiced treatment of the black community based on race and restrictions on their use of institutions (schools, churches, and hospitals) and public facilities (parks, playgrounds, toilets, and restaurants). This period also saw the birth and expansion of the Ku Klux Klan—a white supremacist organization. With the Klan, lynching became a 'routine response' to any form of black self-assertion, be it to acquire education, social and political equality or cultural inclusion. Educated blacks were especially vulnerable. Stories and episodes of lynching instilled such terror in the heart and minds of the blacks that it ensured their acquiescence to white domination. This period, known in US history as Jim Crow—which was originally a song-and-dance caricature to mock black people but by the end of the nineteenth century came to refer to the legal institutionalization of racism—left a dark legacy of several thousand black people lynched to death.

How did the majority of white people respond to these lynchings? The reactions ranged from absolute cold revulsion, hostile defensiveness to collective amnesia. One would imagine that it was the mob murder that inspired horror. But it didn't. What struck terror in white hearts was the supposed crime of the black man—the rape of white women. At the core of lynching was the white fear of lustful black men as rapists of white women. This is vividly captured in Harper Lee's novel *To Kill a Mockingbird* (1960). The 'defenseless white woman' was the centrepiece of pro-lynching propaganda. No amount of consensual sex between the two races could remove the paranoia of the majority community. Seen from the perspective of white people, the victim was not the lynched black man or the white woman but the white man whose woman had been supposedly violated. The black man was assumed to be guilty in every story. When allowed to speak before being lynched, black men were known to confess their guilt, beg for forgiveness, at times protest their innocence or to simply call upon God for mercy. Lynching thus entrenched the white supremacists' sense of being historical victims and in turn criminalized the black men.

Lynching wasn't just any other murder. Lynching, where a mob captures, drags, maims, and hangs another human is very much like gang rape in its symbolism. In many cases, the genitalia of the men was mutilated or they were castrated. Gang rape and lynching are both about male power and privilege over the victim's body. Lynching, a majoritarian act carried out against the defenceless minority, instead of being seen as such, was presented as an act of self-reclamation guaranteeing the power and privilege of the dominant white male. It thrived on the myth of the 'black male rapist'. Each lynched black man was called the 'big burly black brute'. Lynching restored white honour by righting a perceived wrong—the black aggressor was punished and the patriarchal duty fulfilled. It was a form of collective, retributive justice that the majority community carried out in the name of righting historical injustice. Lynching was a public demonstration, a vivid spectacle of the supposed moral superiority of the majoritarian community. At times the lynchers did not even wear a mask, collected body parts of the lynched as souvenirs, and even took photographs that circulated as postcards.

What accounted for the lynchings? What throttled the moral prohibition against murder and torture? What muzzled the bystanders and the rest of the community? Historical research shows that the lynchings in the US would increase in number each time there was an economic depression. Free black labourers competed with white workers for employment. Lynching was a device to intimidate the blacks and keep them out of job competition. The labour market's instability and a permissive government determined the number of lynchings in a particular region. However, in focusing on extraneous explanations such as macroeconomic forces; the mobilization of perpetrators by ill-intentioned community leaders; the workings of a bureaucratic state that enabled individuals to deflect responsibility (what is also known as the 'banality of evil'); inter-group competition and the struggle for survival, one forgets that lynching is a physical act carried out on humans by other humans. It is the psychological edifice—a way of being, thoughts, and feelings—all intrinsic to one's being that enables an act such as lynching.

Pride in one's race and racial hatred was at the heart of lynchings. People were not empty vessels who could be fooled by politicians into ganging up on the blacks. Neither was it the case that the state coerced people. All it did was to not use its powers to prevent this violence. This wasn't about primordialist or instrumentalist mobilization either. The question of people's motives is a red herring. They did not need a motive. In fact in many cases they had no motive. It is a story of a neutral conscience, untroubled, passive, and dispassionate. It was the firm conviction in one's own racial superiority and a deep hatred for the blacks that made the white people 'willing executioners'. How else can one explain the maiming and brutalization of the victims? The lynchings helped maintain the order of things. It kept racial boundaries in place. It was meant to stymie any possibility of miscegenation—the forbidden sexual intermixing of races. This explains why most white folks who did not participate in the lynchings did little to stop them or did anything to ameliorate the lives of black folks. These were the very people who were capable of love, kindness, and generosity, who went to church, raised families, and supported neighbours. But, in this case, they chose hate as their beacon. But wait, it wasn't just hate. The white people actually feared the freed blacks. It was their fear which was black. The same fear that British planters felt around Indian servants; the fear that Afrikaners felt living in their compounds in South Africa; the fear that French army men felt living in Algeria; the fear that white settlers felt in Kenya. It was their fear that made them lash out, kill, maim, and brutalize. It won them the deference and submission of the blacks. Lynching was a way white folks protected themselves as they would from 'yellow fever and the malaria—the work of noxious insects'. This made them feel safe. No law was ever made that brought the lynchers to justice.

In Jim Crow, the acts of witnessing lynchings as bystanders or through the medium of newspapers, pamphlets, ballads, popular stories, photographs, postcards, and cinema lent the white people a sense of security. The photographs carried images of lynched bodies stripped, burnt, mutilated, contorted, desecrated, and bullet-ridden, hung from trees, telephone poles, gallows, bridges or barn rafters. The photographs of white voyeurs and spectators around the dead bodies rarely ever showed any horror. Many of them could be seen smiling and jostling to get inside the camera's frame. The others gazed proudly at the camera. They could have been at a baseball game, a rock concert or at an open-air movie theatre. Workers got half-day leave to attend the lynching. Parents sent notes to school, recalling their children so they could view lynchings. Families attended lynchings with children atop their parents' shoulders. A nine-year old child returning from a viewing complained to his mom: 'I have seen a man hanged, now I wish I could see one burned.' The supremacist violence was a normal aspect of people's lives. The torture and mutilation of blacks was passed off as a legitimate customary practice. What one saw was the growing perversion of the white community which abetted, sanctified, and at times celebrated the lynchings primarily through its deafening silence. In this way lynching bound the white community across class, generational, and geographical divides. Each and every white person was silently complicit. W. E. B. Du Bois raged against this silence in his autobiography: 'One could not be a calm, cool, and detached scientist, while Negroes were lynched, murdered, and starved.' Lynching did not leave any possibility of a neutral stance—or for silence. However, many kept silent. Mark Twain, a contemporary of Du Bois, whom we know as the writer of *The Adventures of Tom Sawyer*, wrote a blistering essay in 1901, titled 'The United States of Lyncherdom' as a reaction to a newspaper account of a lynching. Twain insisted in his essay that the lynchers were assassins and ought to be executed. Nonetheless, he never published the essay. Twain preferred to remain silent because he believed that he would not have even 'half a friend' left once it was published. He would rather have his friends than speak up for the oppressed. This was the affective community of violence.

Might we read the repugnant history of the lynching of black people as a parable of our times? In India, the majoritarian community deploys lynching time and again as a weapon against Dalits and religious minorities in the name of restoring its honour. Lynching has almost acquired the form of a legitimate customary practice with 'beef' vigilante groups roaming through city streets. Political analysts and social scientists describe this as a new phenomenon in Indian politics. However, is it really the case that India is gradually becoming indifferent to or tolerant of the violence because of its excess? The evidence says otherwise. The stories of Shambhuka, Barbareek, Bali, Eklavya, and Karna illustrate how India has always been tolerant of such violence. Each act of lynching entrenches the Hindu supremacist's sense of being a historical victim and in turn criminalizes the Dalit, the Muslim or the Christian man. At the core of every lynching was the Hindu fear of the lustful Dalit or Muslim man who is after the Hindu cow and Hindu women (i.e., enacting Love Jihad). The 'defenceless cow', bechari gai, or 'our mothers, daughters and sisters', hamari ma, betiyaan or behnein, is the centrepiece of pro-lynching propaganda. As a chilling poem in one of the pamphlets circulating in Gujarat in 2002 reminded Hindus: 'The volcano which was inactive for years has erupted.' The supposed victim was the Hindu supremacist whose women had allegedly been violated for centuries. The Dalit or Muslim man was assumed to be guilty in every story. Nothing could remove the paranoia of the majority community. It was interesting to see how violence had been externalized, Othered, and justified in the name of enacting social justice.

EPILOGUE

Babu, did you know as a child what your father did when he was annoyed with his mother? He used to drink up all the milk in the kitchen. Leave none for the family's evening tea. To ensure that your father had enough milk and ghee, his grandfather had bought him a buffalo. So, despite having a buffalo all to himself, he would find excuses to polish off others' share of milk. Your father's love for milk was legendary and even made him the butt of jokes. During college days, when all the boys were going out drinking, your father would stay back nursing a glass of milk. Your father's grandfather, Radhavallabh, was a respected wool trader of his village. He owned herds of sheep and goats that the local shepherds would take for grazing. He lived in Braj in a village called Aryakhera near the city of Mathura. His ancestors had migrated from Rajasthan probably as part of seasonal transhumance with their herd and then stayed on in the region of Mathura. Your great-grandfather got to keep the wool and ewes while the shepherds got the milk. He would sell the wool in the wholesale market in Delhi. The profits from the sale nourished his extended family. In the off-season when they were waiting for the sheep to grow their coats, he supplemented the family income through buying and selling fresh hides. At times the elders in the family would make the kids a drum from the drying hides. Your father had one such drum. It made the sweetest sound. You would have loved it.

Besides milk your father had another favourite food. It was rakti, the fried blood of a freshly slaughtered male goat. Whenever a goat was being slaughtered at the back of the house he would rush out with his bronze thali to collect the flowing blood. He would scurry back to the kitchen with the thali, make sure someone lighted the chulha, and poured the blood in a kadhai. He would stand by the chulha with his mouth watering. The blood would cook into something that looked like a red-coloured egg bhurji. Without waiting for it to cool off, he would polish it right off the kadhai with his fingers. It was a pure delight. A rare delicacy that wasn't available anywhere other than in his mother's kitchen. What made it special was that this was his dish, for him alone. He also loved kheech which was made out of the buffalo's first milk after it had delivered a calf. This milk is yellowish in colour. It was boiled for several hours and then sugar was added to it. It became like chhena, homemade cheese. Although the entire family would savour the kheech, your father had the first right to it because he was the youngest. The other day your father reminded me that he had another favourite dish—goat kidneys, the gurda. They had to be cooked in the hot ashes of the chulha. They would simmer and cook for hours. The kidneys would come out hot and smoking. He would clear the ashes and eat them without adding any salt or pepper. They were smoked, soft, rolled off the tongue, and melted in the mouth. Again a delicacy, and now you know why. It was available only in your grandmother's kitchen. What made it all the more special was that your father had the first right to it. An important variable in a household with several siblings.

In the subcontinent, food, cuisines, dietary habits, what goes on our plates, what gets discarded, rules about what to eat and what not to eat, and when to eat, the seasons of different food items, how to cook, and when to cook, how to serve, which vessels to use—all that goes in the name of eating, feasting, dieting and offerings are tied to one's family, its caste, and the region it comes from. The life of your father's pastoral family was intimately tied to their goats and sheep. For them, the animals were the most important economic resource valuable for their wool, hides, skin, milk, manure, and meat. They were sacred as pashudhan, animal wealth, but not something that could not be consumed. The goats lived in your father's village home as pets, nestling with him on the charpoy, sunning themselves under it, standing around the doorway or frolicking in the passages. At times he would attach a nipple to a bottle and feed a newborn goat. A male lamb or a male goat would be slaughtered whenever there was a celebration or when a mannat, a wish, was fulfilled or when everyone felt like a good meal.

Babu, by the way, did I tell you, your father had his own goat in his Delhi house that his grandfather had brought for him from the village? Your father remembers his goat with such tenderness and ruefully claims that someone stole it for meat. The animals also tied the family into a symbiotic relationship with other artisanal and farming communities in the village. Amma, your father's grandmother, would make yarn out of the wool on her charkha and then give it to the julaha, the weaver, who lived nearby to make 'pure wool' blankets that were the same colour as the fleece on the sheep. In return for grazing the sheep and goats in the village's fields, the nearby farming communities would receive the animal manure which was an important fertilizer for the crops. Grain was bought from the nomadic Banjaras, the traditional carriers of goods (salt and grains) and transporters of cattle and army supplies going back to the Mughal period.

The youngest of five siblings, your father was born under a neem tree. So the joke when we got married was that he was born outdoor and I indoor (since I was born in Indore). Your father was spoilt silly until his little brother was born. By the time the youngest came, his family had already moved to Delhi. As a child growing up in the village your father would spend time running through the fields, bathing under hand pumps, aiming at birds with a catapult, watching the cattle graze, and chasing after his elder siblings. The move to Delhi meant the loss of an idyllic childhood and the lovely culinary delights that village life provided. The visits back to the village during the summer holidays were like the much-awaited rain after a dry spell. But like all things sweet, the holidays went by too quickly. Moving to the big city meant not being able to eat one's favourite foods, except for milk, but also not being able to talk about it to anyone. The family outwardly merged its identity with that of the neighbours, all middle-class professionals. City life came with silences, the blotting out of certain ways of being, and a deep hankering for 'return'. A familiar story amongst all families who migrate.

The stories of pastoral communities have been absent from traditional histories of South Asia. The subcontinent's archaeological records, royal inscriptions, court records, land grants, and epigraphs barely ever mention them. For most of their history the pastoral communities have lived on the margins of dominant sedentary farming communities or state systems. Organized into small communities with little economic and military power, the pastoralists live scattered across India. The ecological reason for the dispersed nature of pastoral communities in South Asia is the absence of vast swathes of pastures or grasslands. This historically annulled the possibility of the rise of big and powerful pastoral communities as in Africa or Central Asia. The pastoralists in India tend to move and live in smaller communities that specialize in one or two animals. It is generally the multi-animal pastoralists who are known to have formed big empires in history—the Ghaznavid, Ghurid, and Genghis Khan's empires are some such examples. The pastoral communities are grouped into different religions—Hindus, Muslims, Christians, and Sikhs. However, the low-caste or outcaste status remains the common denominator.

The way goats and sheep were part of your father's life, cattle are integral to the lives of several artisanal, farming, and pastoral communities. Some cattle-owning communities, probably under the influence of Vaishnavism, began to worship their cattle and stopped consuming them. They would sell their cattle to local butchers once they grew old. However, some cattle-centred communities also consumed their cattle the way your father's family consumed their sheep and goats. The lives of the Mala and Madiga communities, the cobbler and the leather-working castes in southern India, had such an intimate connection with their animals, especially the cattle. Gogu Shyamala, a prominent Telugu writer and women's activist, captures this intimacy in one of her poems:

> To this day
> have you reared a pair of bullocks?
> A pair of sheep? A buffalo or two?
> Have you driven them to the forest to graze?
> Have you at least reared a pair of fowl?
>
> Have you once waded into the stream
> to scrub and wash their bulk?
> You've never plumbed a bullock's ear,
> nor do you know the number of its teeth.
> Don't know the medicine for its toothache,
> don't know to trim its painful hooves!
> Do you know of cattle fuzz?
> What, in the end, do you know
> my friend, but to say 'don't eat beef'?
>
> For her daughter at whose breast
> a newborn child sucks; for that
> just-delivered mother,
> fine cut and pounded beef
> anxious Yellamma plans to get.
> Scan the village length and breadth
> for that elusive sac of bovine bile that hangs

Maybe from Mala Sattemma's rafter or
Madiga Ellamma's beam.
To soothe a baby's gripe,
cure elders' ills and aches
they trust the bile sac's bitter nectar.
And you dare tell them 'Don't eat beef'?
They will reach for their old chappals, take speed!
...

The culture of our cattle fairs
every ten kilometres—across
Dakkhan, (Telangana, Andhra, Maharashtra,
Karnataka)
Malnad, Mangalur, Chittoor, Nellore, Ongole and
Aurangabad, stand
and see the fair stretch in all directions,
cows, calves, bulls and oxen on every side.
The world knows of cowboys, what
does it know of these fairs?
Behind them
do you know who slogs and sweats?
....

You have copied Buddhism's stripes.
Don't we know Buddhism?
It said 'don't kill humans'.
You say 'don't eat mutton, beef, onions and garlic'.
Saying 'we don't eat meat' you are ready to slash and
murder men.
Who are you to speak of animals—you

who have no humanity, no civilization?
The ox, the cow, the bull and buffalo
are members of our families.
What they need we know to grow,
what they suffer we know to treat.
Neuter them and make them work—we do this.
Go to the Mala Madiga wada and learn!

We have created civilization there.
Have you forgotten that our country was born of
this?
Ecology and civilization is our nature.
War and destruction, your culture.
Your relation to the cow is limited:
Milk, sweets, vegetarianism!

Cattle were integral not only to the communities that lived with them but also in the economic and cultural world beyond. You know, even the 'king of percussion instruments', the mridangam, wears a crown of cow hide. The double-headed leather drum has been an integral part of Carnatic music and Tamil-Brahmin culture for centuries. Mridangam-makers in southern India have traditionally been Dalit or Dalit converts to Christianity. Without them and cow hide there would be no mridangam and no Carnatic music. Neither would there be maddalams, an important percussion instrument used in Kerala's dance drama, Kathakali, and the percussion orchestra, panchavadyam. Known as 'divya vadya', a divine instrument, the maddalam is made in Palakkad district in Kerala by the Kadaiyans, a Dalit caste. They specialize in making the maddalam and other percussion instruments such as the tabla, chenda, and edakka. Cow hide would eventually also make possible the game of cricket, the 'national religion' of India. Cricket balls are made of cow hide. Cricket ball manufacturers procure hides from 'states like Kerala, West Bengal, Arunachal Pradesh, Mizoram, Meghalaya, Nagaland, Tripura, and Sikkim where cow slaughter is legal'.

The Mala and Madiga community members when they moved out of their villages into towns and cities carried with them their food habits or at least their gastronomical desires. In the coastal Guntur district of Andhra Pradesh, the distinguishing aspect of the community of Bethany Christians who had converted from Mala and Madiga castes, was beef-eating. They believed that beef consumption set them apart from their pre-conversion past and from the 'Hindus'. In their community, the consumption of beef symbolically provided social cohesion and was a celebration of a shared identity. Beef-consumption was also a means of regaining self-respect as it was associated with progressiveness and modernity. Feasting on cattle was no longer a marker of ritual impurity (seen as such by the upper-caste Hindus) but a sign of respectability and of social morality unfettered by traditions. Further down south, the Syrian Christians of Kerala are also known as the fish, pork, and beef-eating Christians. In north-eastern India as well, beef was the commonest food amongst the different Naga tribes. This is attested by Naga scholars and in the works of British officials stationed in the Naga Hills and Assam such as J. H. Hutton and J. P. Mills.

Slaughtering a live, well-fed animal and enjoying its meat

was very different in tenor from communities who ate dead cattle or animals that were considered inedible by most others (rats, lizards, dogs, chicken feet, chicken intestines, bee larvae, and epiglottis of goats) or coarse grains (jowar or sorghum, ragi, and bajra) or the jhoothan, or leftover or discarded food or use of animal fat for cooking because of lack of ghee or other oils. This was true of several untouchable and forest communities who were considered beyond the pale of the varna system. Dalit autobiographies, poetry, and songs talk about how their food was impacted by their existential realities. Daya Pawar in his book, *Baluta,* describes the elation when a dead cow was brought into the village. The encircling vultures would help them spot a dead animal. The Mahars would rush to the carcass, competing with vultures and birds. They would joyously skin the cow and distribute the meat to the entire community. Sometimes a fight would break out for the cherished bones, the ones above the knees and the back. He would relish chanya, the crispy strips of smoked and roasted beef. Having a cache of chanya in your home was a marker of pride. Eating beef was a delight not only because it was a delicacy but also because of its rarity. The rarity of being able to fill your stomach. Hunger was a dominant aspect of Dalit lives. 'Give us this Day a Feast of Flesh', a poem by N. D. Rajkumar, a poet and a musician who used to work as a daily wage labourer in the Railway Mail Service in Nagercoil, captures this hunger that was interspersed with brief and fleeting moments of feasting:

We eat frogs to calm
That wheezing breath
To cure the fit
We wash cat flesh
In running water
And eat it happily
Like the undead...

We fuck the devil
While our blood runs
And runs...
We capture the devil
In the cage of our hearts...
We keep the spine from collapsing
With chopped cow's tail
Soup drunk as if it is
Made from the leg bones
Of the goat...
The pork fat that cures
Piles, the wound healing
Soup brought by the Araki
Will arouse me...
While we eat this food
As medicine and offerings to our Gods
The roadside shops
Surrounded with
Scattered fish bones
And beef for Sunday dinner

The Mahar community got its name from mrutahari, people who eat the dead. The Musahars of Bihar got their name from being rat-eaters. Their food gave them their identity. They say that the Vedas call this food tamasik—filthy, putrid, and filled with darkness. The food, physical appearance, colour of skin and eyes, texture of hair, and the entire physiognomy and the naming of a community were all ways of marking the difference between the self and the Other. A difference that mutated into a marker of superiority and inferiority, purity and impurity, saatvik and tamasik, the honest and the criminal, honourable and shameful. And then social rituals developed around these misanthropic differences in order to firmly hold them in place. The texts of the Great Tradition commanded: 'You shall not have sexual relations with the Other, you shall not love the Other, you shall not marry the Other, you shall not procreate with the Other for the other is heen, tuchch, Mleccha, asprishya, achchoot.' But is it the food or the people who were tamasik? Perhaps being born out of the feet of Brahma made them filthy. Were they filthy or were Brahma's feet filthy? Who assigned the names Mahar and Musahar to those communities? How come the meat-eating Kayasthas or the Kashmiri, Hussaini (Muhial), and Pirali Brahmins don't have pejorative community names?

Maintaining purity was the principle for endogamy, marrying within one's jati (but outside of one's gotra). The reformists cried themselves hoarse prescribing dining together and intermarriage as a way of breaking down these caste boundaries. But when did a Brahmin eat in Dalitwada? Or when was the last time 'Indian' food included Dalit culinary delights? Or when did we ever see a Dalit female nationalist icon in our school textbooks, not to speak of the near absence of Dalits in academia, judiciary, bureaucracy, journalism, and the legislature? The Aryan and the non-Aryan rarely ate, slept or lived together. If they ever did so, it was under cover, masked, clothed, and disguised; or on the terms set by the dvija. Union between the two sides was forbidden; anyone who dared to break the injunction ran the risk of being shamed, ostracized, dishonoured, raped or even murdered if found out.

So Babu, your parents' story is one of miscegenation. Both Bharmall and Barbareek were your ancestors. Your father and I embodied them and now you do. This is your inheritance. Inheritance by definition is not always of your choosing. But while you are tethered to it, you are no way bound by it. You are free to choose the elements of your inheritance that you wish to own, to discard, to celebrate, to be indifferent to, or even to fight. Your inheritance will acquire the meaning you give it.

ACKNOWLEDGEMENTS

This book was brewing for twenty years. I am grateful to Aienla Ozukum for gently nudging it out of me. Thank you for your friendship, the books, and the meals we have shared. My gratitude to David Davidar for believing in me. My thanks to Bena Sareen for the lovely cover design.

I thank Professor Nonica Datta of the Centre for Historical Studies, JNU, Dr Mayak Kumar of Satyawati College, Professor Rita Kothari of Ashoka University, and eminent journalist Mr Zafar Agha for guidance, critical comments, and encouragement; and my cousin Shubham Vaidik for helping me with Babaji's book collection.

I am grateful to my friend Charu Dua for being a patient and a critical listener to early drafts of the book and for being the most affable travel companion. My thanks to her and Prashant for their loving support. Thanks to Carole Sargent for being my cheerleader. To Gwen Kelly for her friendship. To Vijay, I remain indebted for journeying with me.

Thanks to my parents for their love and encouragement. I am grateful that I got a chance to read out parts of the manuscript to my mother before she passed on. Thanks to Anil for being our little family's keeper and nourishing our lives with music, poetry, and laughter. Not so sure about the two little ruffians, Advait Vallabh and Uddhav Pratap, whose rioting, hugs, kisses, and giggles conned poor Sisyphus into letting go of her boulder several times. This book got written despite them.

NOTES AND REFERENCES

CHAPTER 1: THE STORY OF BHARMALL

3   **started plying me with books by an Indore-born Maharashtrian author:** P. N. Oak served in the Indian National Army, worked as a journalist after World War II and thereafter was an official in the Ministry of Information and Broadcasting. According to him, the Kaaba in Mecca and the Taj Mahal were originally Shiva shrines. P. N. Oak, *The Taj Mahal is a Hindu Palace*, Bombay: Pearl Books, 1968.

8   **lived in the region of Braj:** Richard Barz, *The Bhakti Sect of Vallabhacharya*, Delhi: Munshiram Manoharlal, 1992.

9   **Bengal to Braj to spread his message:** Tony K. Stewart, *The Final Word: The Caitanya Caritamrta and the Grammar of Religious Tradition*, New York: Oxford University Press, 2010.

9   **Vaishnavism would flourish in Braj and Gujarat:** Shandip Saha, 'The Movement of Bhakti along a North-West Axis: Tracing the History of the Pushti Marg between the Sixteenth and Nineteenth Centuries', *International Journal of Hindu Studies*, Vol. 11, No. 3, December 2007, pp. 299–318.

10   **seamlessly lauded the Mughal emperors:** Allison Busch, *Poetry of Kings: The Classical Hindi Literature of Mughal India*, New York: Oxford University Press, 2011; Anne-Marie Gaston, 'Continuity of Tradition in the Music of Nathdvara: A Participant-Observer's View', in Karine Schomer et al, eds., *The Idea of Rajasthan: Explorations in Regional Identity*, Vol. 1, Delhi: Manohar, 2001, pp. 238–77; Ramya Sreenivasan, 'Rethinking Kingship and Authority in South Asia: Amber (Rajasthan), ca. 1560–1615, *Journal of the Economic and Social History of the Orient*, Vol. 57, No. 4, 2014, pp. 549–86;

Norbert Peabody, 'In Whose Turban Does the Lord Reside?: The Objectification of Charisma and the Fetishism of Objects in the Hindu Kingdom of Kota', *Comparative Studies in Society and History*, Vol. 33, No. 4, 1991, pp. 726–54.

11   **they would continue to enjoy pre-eminence:** Tryna Lyons, *The Artists of Nathdwara: The Practice of Painting in Rajasthan*, Bloomington: Indian University Press, 2004; Peter Bennett, *The Path of Grace: Social Organisation and Temple Worship in a Vaishnava Sect*, Delhi, India: Hindustan Publishing Corporation, 1993; Shandip Saha, *Creating a Community of Grace: A History of the Pushti Marga in Northern and Western India (1479–1905)*, PhD thesis submitted at the University of Ottawa, 2004.

12   **Cattle (cows, oxen and bulls) were an important form of wealth:** Mayank Kumar, *Monsoon Ecologies: Irrigation, Agriculture and Settlement Patterns in Rajasthan During the Pre-Colonial Period*, New Delhi: Manohar, 2013.

12   **Rajput ruler's association with the image of Krishna:** Nonica Datta, *Forming an Identity: A Social History of the Jats*, New Delhi: Oxford University Press, 1999; Rajshree Dhali, 'Popular Religion in Rajasthan: A Study of Four Deities and their Worship in Nineteenth and Twentieth Century', PhD Thesis, Jawaharlal Nehru University, 2004, available at <http://shodhganga.inflibnet.ac.in/handle/10603/15372> [accessed: 9 July 2019]; Dhali, 'Pilgrimage to the Abode of a Folk Deity', in *International Journal of Religious Tourism and Pilgrimage*, Vol. 4, No. 6, 2016, pp. 33–41; Norman P. Ziegler, 'Evolution of the Rathore State of Marvar: Structural Change and Warfare', in Karine Schomer et al (eds.), *The Idea of Rajasthan: Explorations in Regional Identity*, Vol. 2, Delhi: Manohar, 2001, pp. 193–201.

12   **A shrine is built where his body falls off the horse:** Rustom Bharucha, *Rajasthan: An Oral History—Conversations with Komal Kothari*, New Delhi: Penguin Books, 2015, p. 106.

13   **Many of the jujhar deities were Rajputs:** Ibid; Pemaram, *Madhyakaleen Rajasthan mein Dharmik Andolan*, Ajmer: Archana Prakashan, 1977; Datta, *Forming an Identity*.

13 **by the nineteenth century he acquires a firm Rajput identity:** Datta, *Forming an Identity*; Harjot Oberoi, *The Construction of Religious Boundaries: Culture, Identity and Diversity in Sikh Tradition*, Chicago: University of Chicago Press, 1994; Sumit Guha, 'Forest Polities and Agrarian Empires: The Khandesh Bhils, c. 1700–1850', in *Indian Economic and Social History Review*, Vol. 33, No. 2, 1996, pp. 133–53.

14 **She is worshipped in different parts of Rajasthan:** Bharucha, *Rajasthan*, p. 140.

15 **Muslim butcher in the tale belonged to:** See Madhav Gadgil and Kailash Malhotra, 'Ecology of a Pastoral Caste: Gavli Dhangars of Peninsular India', *Human Ecology*, Vol. 10, No. 1, 1982, pp. 107–43; M. L. K. Murthy and Günther D. Sontheimer, 'Prehistoric Background to Pastoralism in the Southern Deccan in the Light of Oral Traditions and Cults of some Pastoral Communities', *Anthropos*, 1980, pp. 163–84.

15 **Although the Dhangar subgroup converted to Islam:** Asiya Siddiqi, 'Ayesha's World: A Butcher's Family in Nineteenth-Century Bombay', *Comparative Studies in Society and History*, Vol. 43, No. 1, June 2001, pp. 101–29.

17 **continued to maintain their social or caste location:** Richard Eaton, 'Approaches to Study of Conversion to Islam in India', Richard C. Martin, *Approaches to Islam in Religious Studies*, Tucson: University of Arizona Press, 1985, pp. 106–23; 'The Political and Religious Authority of the Shrine of Baba Farid', in his *Essays on Islam in Indian History*, New Delhi: Oxford University Press, 2000, pp. 203–24; and 'Chapter 5: Mass Conversion to Islam: Theories and Protagonists', in *The Rise of Islam and the Bengal Frontier, 1204-1760*, Berkeley: University of California Press, 1993; Suraj Bhan Bhardwaj, *Contestations and Accommodations: Mewat and Meos in Mughal India*, New Delhi: Oxford University Press, 2016.

18 **'considered exclusively Hindu in India today':** Cynthia Talbot, 'Becoming Turk the Rajput Way: Conversion and Identity in an Indian Warrior Narrative', *Modern Asian Studies*, Vol. 43, No. 1, 2009, pp. 211–43; Rustom Bharucha, 'Muslims and Others: Anecdotes,

Fragments and Uncertainties of Evidence', *Economic and Political Weekly*, Vol. 38, No. 40, 2003, pp. 4238–50.

CHAPTER 2: MY GRANDFATHER—THE ARYAN

20 the Sanskrit language possessed European roots: Romila Thapar, 'The Theory of Aryan Race and India: History and Politics', in her collection of essays titled *Cultural Pasts: Essays in Early Indian History*, New Delhi: Oxford University Press, 2000, pp. 1108–141.

21 The clash between the two was believed to have given rise: Ibid.

22 the announcement of the 'discovery' of the Indus Valley Civilization: Thomas R. Trautmann, 'Introduction', *The Aryan Debate*, New Delhi: Oxford University Press, 2005, pp. xiii–liii.

23 Starting from Raja Ram Mohan Roy to Keshub Chandra Sen: Raja Ram Mohan Roy, Vivekananda, Savarkar differed with others on the issue of beef-eating. Unlike others, they did not condemn it.

24 the need was to first retrieve the golden age: Dorothy M. Figueira, *Aryans, Jews, Brahmins: Theorizing Authority Through Myths of Identity*, New Delhi: Navayana, 2002, 2015.

25 The Aryan civilization's strength thus lay: Vivekananda, *The Complete Works of Swami Vivekananda*, Vol. 11, Advaita Ashram, Calcutta, 1991, p. 159 cited in Figueira, *Aryans*, p. 137.

25 the argument that it was related to birth: The solution was thus sought at the level of practice. An example of this was Gandhi's performance of 'bread labour'. For him, weaving his clothes and cleaning his toilet was a way of doing away with untouchability. For him it was a 'labour' question not as much as an existential question tied to one's birth.

25 Violence was something, therefore, that the Muslims and the British did: Gandhi took this a step further and in his pamphlet *Hind Swaraj* (1909), where he deemed violence to be the essential element of the Western civilization. Upinder Singh in her *Political Violence in Ancient India*, Cambridge: Harvard University Press, 2017, also makes the point that Gandhi and Nehru helped create a myth of non-violence and the way it obscured the political violence in

India's ancient past. She primarily focuses on the history of state violence and its sanctification by the epics, religious texts, aesthetics, inscriptions, and the political narratives.

26 **Dayanand Saraswati wrote *Satyarth Prakash* (The Light of Truth) in 1875:** Swami Dayanand Saraswati, *Satyarth Prakash*, Delhi: Arsh Sahitya Prakash Trust, 1875, 2008 (repr).

26 **'These foreigners took to drinking wine':** Durga Prasad, *English Translation of Satyarth Prakash*, Lahore: Virajnand Press, 1908, pp. 286, 288, and 460.

26 **he also refuted the general impression that the Ashwamedha:** However, he doesn't actually say what these words referred to if not to horse and cow sacrifice. Ibid., pp. 162–63.

26 **Dayanand made persuasive arguments:** Swami Dayanand Saraswati, *Gaukarunanidhi*, Delhi: Arsh Sahitya Prachar Trust, 1881, 1998 (repr).

26 **the slaughter of cows increased the cost of cattle:** Theresa O'Toole, 'Secularizing the Sacred Cow: The Relationship between Religious Reform and Hindu Nationalism', in Antony Copley (ed.), *Hinduism in Public and Private: Reform, Hindutva, Gender and Sampraday*, New Delhi: Oxford University Press, 2003, pp. 84–109.

29 **As the kids were born, Arya Samaji values were instilled:** Swami Vaidikanand, *Swami Dayanand ke Amrit Vachan*, Bhaag 2, Indore: Swami Dayanand Brhamgyan Ashram Nyas, 2007, 4th edition, pp. 4–7.

30 **The Arya Samaj thus offered a new community:** Datta, *Forming an Identity*.

CHAPTER 3: THE COW PROTECTION MOVEMENT

32 **diluted the hostile objections of the traditional Hindu priests:** Sandra Freitag, 'Sacred Symbol as Mobilizing Ideology: The North Indian Search for a "Hindu" Community', *Comparative Studies in Society and History*, Vol. 22, No. 4, October 1980, pp. 597–625.

32 **They used the local melas or fairs and festivals:** Ibid; Peter Robb, 'The Challenge of Gau Mata: British Policy and Religious Change in India, 1880–1916', *Modern Asian Studies*, Vol. 20, No. 2, 1986, pp. 285–319.

33   **They could help set up a gaushala:** Anand A. Yang, 'Sacred Symbol and Sacred Space in Rural India: Community Mobilization in the "Anti-Cow Killing" Riot of 1893', *Comparative Studies in Society and History*, Vol. 22, No. 4, 1980, pp. 576–96; Gyanendra Pandey, *The Construction of Communalism in Colonial North India*, New Delhi: Oxford University Press, 1990, 2006 (repr).

33   **All of them, in turn, exploited the existing fissures:** Freitag, 'Sacred Symbol'.

35   **Many tracts and magazines such as *Gausewak*:** Charu Gupta, 'The Icon of Mother in Late Colonial North India: "Bharat Mata", "Matro Bhasha" and "Gau Mata"', *Economic and Political Weekly*, Vol. 36, No. 45, 2001, pp. 4291–99. Some other texts include Achalram Maharaj, *Hindu Dharma Rahasya*, Agra, 1939 and Dahyabhai Jani, *Romance of the Cow*, Bombay: The Bombay Humanitarian League, 1938.

37   **Hindu selfhood came to be intimately tied to the protection of the cow:** Charu Gupta, 'Articulating Hindu Masculinity and Femininity: "Shuddhi" and "Sangathan" Movements in United Provinces in the 1920s', *Economic and Political Weekly*, Vol. 33, No. 13, 26 March–3 April 1998, pp. 727–35.

37   **this image first appeared in Azamgarh district in 1894:** Christopher Pinney, 'The Nation (Un)Pictured? Chromolithography and "Popular" Politics in India, 1878–1995', *Critical Inquiry*, Vol. 23, No. 4, Summer 1997, pp. 834–67.

37   **did not undertake even the tanning of cow or buffalo hide:** Raibahadur Munshi Hardyalsingh, *Report Mardumshumari Rajmarwaad, 1891: Rajasthan ki Jatiyon ka Itihas evam Ritiriwaaz*, Jodhpur: Maharaj Mansingh Pustak Prakash Shodh Kendra, 1894, 2010, pp. 548.

38   **'Our sexually unsatisfied widows are especially prone':** Manan Dwivedi, *Humara Bhishan Haas*, 1924, cited in Gupta, *Articulating Hindu*, p. 733.

38   **Ai Aryon kyon so rahe ho pair pasare:** *Arya Patra*, week ending 12 July 1924, Native Newspaper Reports Published in the United Provinces cited in Gupta, *Articulating Hindu*, p. 731.

39   **Christian missionaries were able to convert:** Charu Gupta, 'Intimate Desires: Dalit Women and Religious Conversion in Colonial India', *The Journal of Asian Studies*, Vol. 73, No. 3, 2014, pp. 661–87, 664, and 667.

40   **A pomegranate can never change into a guava:** Bandhu Samaj, *Hinduon ki Tez Talwar*, Kanpur: Arya Samaj, 1927, pp. 5–14, cited in Gupta, *Intimate Desires*, p. 666; Gupta's translation.

40   **Image 5: Converted and Unconverted Dalits:** Vyanga Chitravali, Allahabad, 1930, cited in Charu Gupta, 'Feminine, Criminal or Manly: Imaging Dalit Masculinities in Colonial North India' in *Indian Economic and Social History Review*, Vol. 47, No. 3, 2010, pp. 309–42, 334.

41   **caricatures of Dalit men were an acknowledgement:** Ibid.

42   **Panditji and Ghisuva are together taking water from the tap:** Baijnath Kedia, *Vyanga Chitravali*, Part I, Kashi: Hindi Pustak Agency, 1933, p. 34 cited in Gupta, *Intimate Desires*, p. 666, translation mine.

42   **several Brahmins opposed shuddhi of the lower castes:** Gupta, *Intimate Desires*.

43   **opened up the 'Hindu' identity:** Datta, *Forming an Identity*.

44   **Jats, the peasant-pastoral community of North India:** Vijay Parshad, *Untouchable Freedom: A Social History of Dalit Community*, New Delhi: Oxford University Press, 2000; Datta, *Forming an Identity*; and Kalyani Devaki Menon, *Everyday Nationalism: Women of the Hindu Right in India*, Philadelphia: University of Pennsylvania Press, 2012.

45   **cultural Arabization of Indian Islamic practices:** Richard Eaton, 'Approaches to Study of Conversion to Islam in India', in Richard C. Martin, *Approaches to Islam in Religious Studies*, Tucson: University of Arizona Press, 1985, pp. 106–23 and his *The Rise of Islam and the Bengal Frontier, 1204–1760*, Berkeley: University of California Press, 1993.

45   **there also existed deep intra-community and sectarian conflict:** William R. Pinch, 'Soldier Monks and Militant Sadhus', in *Making*

India Hindu: Religion, Community, and the Politics of Democracy in India, New Delhi: Oxford University Press, 1996, pp. 140–61.

CHAPTER 4: VIOLENCE FORGES COMMUNITY

46 **bodies pressing together and breathing in union:** Stanley J. Tambiah, 'Some Reflections on Communal Violence in South Asia', *Journal of Asian Studies*, Vol. 49, No. 4, 1990, pp. 741–60 and his *Leveling Crowds: Ethnonationalist Conflicts and Collective Violence in South Asia*, Berkeley: University of California Press, 1996; Elias Canetti, *Crowds and Power*, New York: Continuum, 1960, 1973 (repr).

48 **began to take the form of 'anti-cow killing' riots:** Freitag, 'Sacred Symbol', 1980; G. R. Thursby, *Hindu-Muslim Relations in British India: A Study of Controversy, Conflict, and Communal Movements in Northern India, 1923–1928*, Leiden: Brill, 1975; Robb, 'Challenge of Gau Mata', 1986, p. 296; Sumit Sarkar, *Modern India: 1885–1947*, Gurgaon: Macmillan, 1983, 2013, p. 60 (repr).

49 **several sanyasis from different monastic traditions and sampradayas:** Walter Hauser and Kailash Chandra Jha, *My Life's Struggle: A Translation of Swami Sahajanand Sarawati's Mera Jivan Sangharsh*, New Delhi: Manohar, 2016, p. 159; Walter Hauser, *The Bihar Provincial Kisan Sabha 1929-1942: A Study of an Indian Peasant Movement*, New Delhi: Manohar, 2019; Lata Singh, 'The Bihar Kisan Sabha Movement-1933-1939', *Social Scientist*, Vol. 20, No. 5/6, 1992, pp. 21–33; S. K. Mittal and Kapil Kumar, 'Baba Ram Chandra and Peasant Upsurge in Oudh: 1920-21', *Social Scientist*, Vol. 6, No. 11, 1978, pp. 35-56; Prem Narain Agrawal, *Bhawani Dayal Sannyasi: A Public Worker of South Africa*, U. P.: The Indian Colonial Association, 1939.

50 **It refers to an instrumentalist use of religion:** Peter van der Veer, *Religious Nationalism: Hindus and Muslims in India*, New Delhi: Oxford University Press, 1994, p. 30.

50 **The British were therefore cautious in their approach:** Yang, 'Sacred Symbol and Sacred Space'.

51 **this led to the outbreak of 'cholera morbus':** W. H. Sleeman,

Rambles and Recollections of an Indian Official, New Delhi: Oxford University Press, 1893, 1915, p. 168 (repr).

51   **another incident where cow slaughter and beef-eating:** Ibid., pp. 193–94, 202–04.

52   **only ethnographic account in his view that captured the Hindu's devotion:** William Crooke, 'The Veneration of the Cow in India,' *Folklore*, 1912, pp. 275–306.

52   **the success of the movement in this sphere was limited:** O'Toole also makes this point; so does Durga Prasad, *Satyarth Prakash*, p. 51.

52   **The British held on to a policy of neutrality:** Yang, 'Sacred Symbol'; Sandra Freitag, 'Natural Leaders, Administrators and Social Control: Communal Riots in the United Provinces', 1870-1925,' *South Asia*, Vol. 1, No. 2, pp. 27–41; Robb, 'The Challenge of Gau Mata'; Ian Copland, 'What to Do about Cows? Princely versus British Approaches to a South Asian Dilemma', *Bulletin of the School of Oriental and African Studies*, London: University of London, Vol. 68, No. 1, 2005, pp. 59–76.

53   **stated that the 'cow' was not a sacred object:** Sandra Freitag, 'Contesting in Public: Colonial Legacies and Contemporary Communalism', in David Ludden (ed.), *Making India Hindu: Religion, Community, and the Politics of Democracy in India*, New Delhi: Oxford University Press, 1996, pp. 211–34.

54   **a wide gap between administrative policies and actual practice:** Ibid; Copland, 'What To Do about Cows?'; Robb, 'The Challenge of Gau Mata'; Thursby, *Hindu-Muslim Relations*.

54   **People saw the insertion of this article as a compromise:** Article 48 of the Constitution of India: 'Organisation of agriculture and animal husbandry: The State shall endeavour to organise agriculture and animal husbandry on modern and scientific lines and shall, in particular, take steps for preserving and improving the breeds, and prohibiting the slaughter, of cows and calves and other milch and draught cattle'. See Shraddha Chigateri, 'Negotiating the "Sacred" Cow: Cow Slaughter and the Regulation of Difference in India', in M.

Mookherjee (ed.), Studies in Global Justice 7, *Democracy, Religious Pluralism and the Liberal Dilemma of Accommodation*, 2012, pp. 137–59.

55   **in response to the central government's ban:** Prabash K. Dutta, 'Is Ban on Sale of Cattle for Slaughter Unconstitutional: A Fact Check', *India Today*, 16 June 2017; Bhadra Sinha, 'Cattle Trade for Slaughter: Supreme Court Suspends ban Across India', *Hindustan Times*, 12 July 2017.

55   **The politico-legal tussle continues as the majority of Indian states:** 'The States where Cow Slaughter is Legal in India' in *Indian Express,* 8 October 2015.

56   **the Baniya community prevailed over the maharaja:** Robb, 'The Challenge of Gaumata', p. 294; Copland, 'What To Do About the Cows?', p. 62.

57   **I could hear my grandfather bending over and asking:** The *Satyarth Prakash* exhorts the father of the bride to gift a cow to the groom.

58   **Mother Teresa was 'nark ka farishta':** See Image 9 on p. 60.

CHAPTER 5: THE INVISIBILITY OF VIOLENCE

65   **We were also informed that although the temple was named:** Subhash 'Bedhadak', *Sampurna Khatu Shyam Itihaas*, Jaipur: Roodmal Bookseller, undated (possibly 2003 as gleaned from its content).

67   **In some other tales Barbareek appears as Bhima's son:** Ibid., *Skanda Purana*, Maheshwarkhand-Kumarikakhand, Gorakhpur: Gita Press, undated; Devdutt Pattanaik, *Jaya: An Illustrated Retelling of the Mahabharata*, New Delhi: Penguin Books, p. 106.

67   **Like most mythological or literary characters:** Robert Darnton, 'Peasant Tell Tales: The meaning of Mother Goose', *The Great Cat Massacre: and other Episodes in French Cultural History*, New York: Basic Books, 2009, 1999, pp. 9–74 (repr); A. K. Ramanujan, 'Three Hundred Ramayanas: Five Examples and Three Thoughts on Translation,' in Vinay Dharwadker (ed.), *The Collected Essays of A. K. Ramanujan*, New Delhi: Oxford University Press, 1999, pp.

131–60; Romila Thapar, *Sakuntala: Texts, Readings, Histories*, New York: Columbia University Press, 2011; Ramya Sreenivasan, *Many Lives of Rajput Queen: Heroic Pasts in India, c. 1500–1900*, Seattle: University of Washington Press, 2007.

68 **Krishna then blessed Barbareek:** *Skanda Purana*, pp. 233–36.

68 **The first could save anything, the second could destroy anything:** The meaning of the three arrows also keeps changing in different stories. In another version, the first arrow is for the Pandavas, the second for Kauravas and the third for Krishna. See Devdutt Pattanaik, *Shyam: An Illustrated Retelling of the Bhagavata*, New Delhi: Penguin Books, p. 228.

68 **Barbareek was dismayed that he would not be able to see:** Devdutt Pattanaik, *Jaya*, pp. 384–89. There are variations of this tale where, instead of the mirror, Krishna uses the ruse that the head of the mightiest warrior had to be sacrificed in order for them to appease the gods before beginning the battle. Barbareek comes forward and offers his head willingly.

69 **Krishna suggested that they consult Barbareek:** According to Alf Hiltebeitel, in another variant is Iravan, Arjuna's son with Ulupi, who is the talking head. See Vishwa Adluri and Joydeep Bagchee, *When the Goddess was a Woman: Mahabharata Ethnographies–Essays by Alf Hiltebeitel*, Vol. 2, Leiden: Brill, 2011, pp. 247–49.

69 **replete with tales and descriptions of foreign invasions:** F. E. Pargiter, *Ancient Indian Historical Tradition*, London: Oxford University Press, 1922.

70 **Image 13: Barbareek observing the battle:** Subhash 'Bedhadak', *Sampurna Khatu Shyam Itihaas*, p. 91.

71 **In a similar vein, Tantric practices began:** B. D. Chattopadhyaya, 'Origin of the Rajputs: The Political, Economic and Social Processes in Early Medieval Rajasthan', in his *The Making of Early Medieval India*, New Delhi: Oxford University Press, 1994, 2001, pp. 59–92; Surajit Sinha, 'State Formation and the Rajput Myth in Central India; *Man in India*, Vol. 42, No. 1, 1964, pp. 36–80; David Hardiman, 'Power in the Forest: The Dangs 1820-1940', in David Arnold and

David Hardiman (eds.), *Subaltern Studies VIII*, New Delhi: Oxford University Press, 1994, pp. 89–147.

71   **similar trajectory of being a non-Aryan deity and later undergoing Rajputization:** Dhali, 'Pilgrimage to the Abode of a Folk Deity', 2016, pp. 33–34; Kunal Chakrabarti, *Religious Process: The Puranas and the Making of a Religious Tradition,* New Delhi: Oxford University Press, 2001.

72   **They legitimate social institutions and practices:** Percy S. Cohen, 'Theories of Myth,' *Man*, New Series, Vol. 4, No. 3, September 1969, pp. 337–53.

72   **Mleccha or barbarian is a pejorative term used for 'foreigners':** Aloka Parasher-Sen, '"Foreigner" and "Tribe" as Barbarian (*Mleccha*) in Early North India', *Subordinate and Marginal Groups in Early India*, New Delhi: Oxford University Press, 2004, pp. 275–313. Mleccha, Yavana and Turushka are used interchangeably for Muslims. See in the same volume Brajadulal Chattopadhyaya, 'Representing the Other? Sanskrit Sources and the Muslims (Eight to Fourteenth Century)', pp. 374–404.

72   **his father Ghatotkacha says:** *Skanda Purana*, Maheshwarkhand-Kumarikakhand, Gorakhpur: Gita Press, undated, p. 224.

72   **In other folktales Barbareek's hair is likened to snakes:** According to Baccha Singh Mahoba, a folk singer of the epic *Alha,* cited in Adluri and Bagchee, *When the Goddess was a Woman*, Vol. 2, Leiden: Brill, 2011, p. 249.

73   **Image 14: Barbareek offering his head to Lord Shyam:** Subhash 'Bedhadak', *Sampurna Khatu Shyam Itihaas*, p. 86.

75   **'You do not really die through this, nor are you harmed':** Rig Veda 1.162.21 cited in Brian K. Smith and Wendy Doniger, 'Sacrifice and Substitution: Ritual Mystification and Mythical Demystification', Numen, Vol. 36, Fasc. 2, December, 1989, pp. 189–224, p. 210.

78   **Valmiki depicted the monkeys as beholden:** Valmiki is seen as betraying his low-caste identity in the modern Dalit literature. See Daya Pawar's poem, 'Oh! Great Poet' (translated by Graham Smith) in Sanjay Paswan and Pramanshi Jaideva (eds.), *Encyclopaedia of*

Dalits in India, Vol. 11, Delhi: Kalpaz Publications, 2002, pp. 106–07.

79   **a radical proposition for an untouchable to have entered a temple:** Patton Burchett, 'Bhakti Rhetoric in the Hagiography of 'Untouchable' Saints: Discerning Bhakti's Ambivalence on Caste and Brahminhood', *International Journal of Hindu Studies*, Vol. 13, No. 2, August 2009, pp. 115–41; Jayashree B. Gokhale-Turner, 'Bhakti or Vidroha: Continuity and Change in Dalit Sahitya', in Jayant Lele (ed.), *Tradition and Modernity in Bhakti Movements*, Leiden: Brill, 1981, pp. 29–42.

80   **Coming out of the communal carnage of the Partition:** Partha Chatterjee and Anjan Ghosh (eds.), *History and The Present*, New Delhi: Permanent Black, 2002; Neeladri Bhattacharya, 'Predicaments of Secular Histories', in *Public Culture*, Vol. 20, No. 1, 2008, pp. 57–73.

80   **past and history were never the same:** Paul Veyne, *Did the Greeks Believe in Their Myths? An Essay on the Constitutive Imagination*, Chicago: University of Chicago Press, 1988.

CHAPTER 6: THE NON-ARYAN UTOPIA

84   **a world that history had, as luck would have it, failed to colonize:** Ashis Nandy, 'History's Forgotten Doubles', *History and Theory*, Vol. 34, No. 2, 1995, pp. 44–66.

85   **The celestial nymphs also came to serve Bali:** Deborah Soifer, *The Myths of Narasimha and Vamana: Two Avatars in Cosmological Perspective*, Albany: State University of New York Press, 1991, p. 121.

86   **'The entire world stood still in nature':** Anand Swarup Gupta, *The Vamana Purana*, Varanasi: All India Kashiraj Trust, 1967, Chapter 24, pp. 112–13.

87   **interrupted the unceasing dynamic:** Deborah Soifer, *The Myths of Narasimha and Vamana*, p. 121.

89   **His writings (a play, ballads, short books, speeches, lectures, and statements):** *Tratiya Ratna* (The Third Eye), 1855, a play, *Chhatrapati Shivaji Raja Bhosale yacha Pavada* (A Ballad of the Raja Chhatrapati Shivaji Bhosale), 1869 and *Brahmanache Kasab* (Priestcraft Exposed,1873) two ballads, *Vidyakhatil Brahman Pantoji*

(Brahman Teachers in the Education Department), 1869, a journal article, *Gulamgiri* (Slavery), 1873, a short book, *Shetkaryaca Asud* (A Cultivator's Whip-Cord), 1883 and *Sarvajanik Satyadharma Pustak* (All the Rites, Ceremonies, and Verses used by the Satyashodhak Samaj), 1887, collections of speeches and lectures and *Memorial Addressed to the Education Commission,* a statement to the Hunter Commission on Education in India in 1882.

90 **writings remind one of the bestselling 'forbidden':** Robert Darnton, *The Forbidden Best-sellers of Pre-Revolutionary France,* London: Fontana Press, 1996.

90 **he took it at face value and mocked it for its absurdity:** Gail Omvedt uses the word empiricisation to describe Jyotiba's treatment of the myths. See her *Seeking Begumpura: The Social Vision of Anticaste Intellectuals,* New Delhi: Navayana, 2008, p. 168.

90 **'Yadi sachmuch mein Brahma ko chaar muha hote':** Jotiba Phule, *Gulamgiri,* L. J. Meshram Vimalkirti, *Jotiba Phule Rachnavali* (Hindi translation), Delhi: Radhakrishan Prakashan, undated, p. 152.

91 **'Phir sawal uthta hai ki uske ghar ka kaam':** Ibid., pp. 151–52.

91 **They go to the extent of condemning Brahma:** Uses the words 'randibaaz' and 'betichod'. See Ibid., p. 152.

91 **Phule denounced the story of Brahma:** Jotiba Phule, *Kisan ke Kode,* in Vimalkirti, *Jotiba Phule Rachnavali,* undated, p. 319.

91 **The utopia was a casteless and just society reminiscent:** Gail Omvedt, *Seeking Begumpura: The Social Vision of Anticaste Intellectuals,* pp. 106–07.

91 **King Bali replaced Ram and Krishna as the puroshottam:** *Gulamgiri,* Chapter 6, pp. 165–68.

92 **a colloquial term of abuse to address the Vaman:** *Gulamgiri,* p. 172–73. Till date, King Bali is celebrated during the harvest festival of Onam amongst the Malayali folks in Kerala and interestingly the Brahmanical version of the festival celebrates the Vaman avatar.

92 **Both imageries appealed to Phule's cultivator-warrior community:** Rosalind O'Hanlon, *Caste, Conflict and Community,* p. 168–75.

92 **Brahmins ensured that Shudras didn't learn to read and write:**

Satyashodhak Samaj, Poona ki Rapat, 20 March 1877, in Vimalkirti, *Jotiba Phule Rachnavali,* pp. 178–79.

93 **Shudra not just referred to a ritually impure caste:** Ibid.

93 **the first to talk of the problems facing India's village economy:** As part of his larger concern for village economy Phule stressed the importance of proper breeding and care of cows and oxen and, like Dayanand, gave economic reasons for banning cow slaughter. See G. P. Deshpande, *Selected Writings of Jotirao Phule,* New Delhi: Leftword Books, 2002, p. 12.

93 **identified the fact that patriarchy and the oppression:** *Jotiba Phule, Tritya Ratna,* 1855, in L. J. Meshram Vimalkirti, *Jotiba Phule Rachnavali* (Hindi Translation), Delhi: Prakashan, undated, pp. 11–50. According to Rosalind O'Hanlon, (in *Caste, Conflict and Community*), there is historical data that bears out Phule's view of the high number of Brahmins in Bombay Presidency's bureaucracy in the 1880s. See Anil Seal, *The Emergence of Indian Nationalism: Competition and Collaboration in the Later Nineteenth Century,* Cambridge: Cambridge University Press, 1968, p. 118.

93 **The students in no time began to shine:** Hari Narke, 'Dnyanajyoti Savitribai Phule I and II', 6 September and 1 October 2012, on *Round Table India,* <http://roundtableindia.co.in/index.php?option=com_content&view=article&id=5681:dnyanajyoti-savitribai-phule-i&catid=115:dalitbahujan-renaissance&Itemid=127> [accessed: 9 July 2019].

94 **The people who dress themselves up and parade round:** Cited in O'Hanlon, *Caste, Conflict and Community,* p. 120.

94 **These were the Ad Dharm movement in Punjab:** Omvedt, *Seeking Begumpura*; M. S. S. Pandian, *Brahmin and Non-Brahmin: Genealogies of the Tamil Political Present,* Ranikhet: Permanent Black, 2007, 2016 (repr); Christophe Jaffrelot, *Dr. Ambedkar and Untouchability: Analysing and Fighting Caste,* London: Hurst, 2000, 2005 (repr).

95 **Why was it that notwithstanding the substantial gains of lower-caste assertion:** O'Hanlon makes this point, p. 150.

96 **Why did the non-Sanskrit and the non-Aryan tradition:** Santosh

Desai, 'Ramayana—An Instrument of Historical Contact and Cultural Transmission between India and Asia', *The Journal of Asian Studies*, Vol. 30, No. 1, November 1970, pp. 5–20.

96 **such loss of symbols and constituency to the larger nationalist mobilization:** Bharat Patankar and Gail Omvedt, 'The Dalit Liberation Movement in Colonial Period', *Economic and Political Weekly*, Vol. 14, No. 7/8, Annual Number: Class and Caste in India, February 1979, pp. 409–11, 413, 415, 417, 419–21, and 423–44; Gail Omvedt, 'Jotirao Phule and the Ideology of Social Revolution in India,' *Economic and Political Weekly*, Vol. 6, No. 37, 11 September 1971, pp. 1969–79; Gail Omvedt, 'The Satyashodhak Samaj and Peasant Agitation', *Economic and Political Weekly*, Vol. 8, No. 44, 3 November 1973, pp. 1971–82; Gail Omvedt, 'Review: Shivaji and Maratha "Swarajya"', *Economic and Political Weekly*, Vol. 24, No. 1, 7 January 1989, pp. 29–30.

97 **nationalist arena didn't have publicly visible and educated lower-caste spokesmen:** Ibid.

97 **When one did receive an education one was either co-opted:** Daya Pawar, *Baluta*, Jerry Pinto (trans.), New Delhi: Speaking Tiger, 2015; Baburao Bagul, *When I Hid my Caste; Stories*, New Delhi: Speaking Tiger, 2018; Arjun Dangle (ed.), *Poisoned Bread*, New Delhi: Orient Blackswan, 2009, 2018 (repr); Omvedt, 'Jotirao Phule', 1971.

CHAPTER 7: THE HISTORICAL VICTIMS

99 **I dived into the post-Independence history of Indore:** Asghar Ali Engineer, 'Communal Frenzy at Indore', *Economic and Political Weekly*, Vol. 24, No. 44/45, 4–11 November 1989, pp. 2467–69; Violet G. J. Galonnier, 'Hindu Muslim Communal Riots in India, II (1986–2011)', 2013, <http://www.sciencespo.fr/mass-violence-war-massacre-resistance/en/document/hindu-muslim-communal-riots-india-ii-1986-2011> [accessed: 9 July 2019].

99 **Television with multiple private channels, the cable network:** Victoria L. Farmer, 'Mass Media: Images, Mobilization, and Communalism', in Ludden, *Making India Hindu*, pp. 98–118; Christiane Brosius, 'Hindutva Intervisuality: Videos and the Politics

of Representation', *Contributions to Indian Sociology*, Vol. 36, No. 1 & 2, 2002, pp. 265–95.

100 **As the procession reached the Ram Laxman Chowk area:** Engineer, 'Communal Frenzy at Indore', p. 2469.

100 **Some local Muslim leaders including the shahar qazi:** Ibid., pp. 2468–69.

101 **This penetration or breach of territoriality by the procession:** Anand A. Yang, 'Sacred Symbol and Sacred Space in Rural India: Community Mobilization in the "Anti-Cow Killing" Riot of 1893', *Comparative Studies in Society and History*, Vol. 22, No. 4, October 1980, pp. 576–96; Richard H. Davis, 'The Iconography of Rama's Chariot', in David Ludden (ed.), *Making India Hindu*, New Delhi: Oxford University Press, 1996, pp. 27–54.

102 **Setting the VHP apart from other organizations:** Peter van der Veer, *Religious Nationalism: Hindus and Muslims in India*, Oxford University Press, 1994, pp. 130–37; Sandria Freitag, 'Contesting in Public: Colonial Legacies and Contemporary Communalism,' in Ludden, *Making India Hindu*, 1996, pp. 211–34.

103 **Ansari was supporting the view taken by Noori:** Tavleen Singh, 'Shah Bano Makes a Dramatic Turnaround', *India Today*, 15 December 1985.

103 **Muslim miscreants on the other hand:** Engineer, 'Communal Frenzy at Indore', p. 2469.

104 **Interestingly similar pattern of the involvement of the lower-caste Hindus:** 'The Khatiks of Kanpur and the Bristle Trade: Towards an Anthropology of man and beast', *Sociological Bulletin*, Vol. 47, No. 2, 1998, pp. 187–206; Paul Brass, *Theft of an Idol: Text and Context in the Representation of Collective Violence*, Princeton: Princeton University Press, 1997, p. 227.

104 **The Sonkars, as specialists in handling pigs and their meat:** Maren Bellwinkel-Schempp, 'Pigs and Power: Urban Space and Urban Decay', in Evelin Hust and Michael Mann (eds.), *Urbanization and Governance in India*, Manohar, New Delhi, 2005, pp. 201–226; 'The Khatiks of Kanpur and the Bristle Trade', 1998, pp. 187–206; and

'Kabir-Panthis in Kanpur: From Sampradaya to Dalit Identity', in Monika Horstmann (ed.), *Images of Kabir*, New Delhi: Manohar, 2002, pp. 215–32. Other than lower-caste Hindus, another segment of population participating actively in these riots were the wrestlers. See Norbert Peabody, 'Disciplining the Body, Disciplining the Body-Politic: Physical Culture and Social Violence among North Indian Wrestlers', *Comparative Studies in Society and History*, Vol. 51, No. 2, April 2009, pp. 372–400.

104 **The Sonkars getting sucked into the VHP maelstrom:** Balmikis are Dalits associated with the work of cleaning toilets, sweeping, and scavenging. The Jats are a traditional agrarian community in northern India. Nonica Datta, 'Hinduisation of the Balmikis', *Economic and Political Weekly*, Vol. 35, No. 41, 7–13 October, 2000, pp. 3655–56. Datta, *Forming an Identity*; Datta, 'Politics of Cow Protection', *The Hindu*, 18 November 2002; Surinder Jodhka and Murli Dhar, 'Cow, Caste and Communal Politics Dalit Killings in Jhajjar', *Economic and Political Weekly*, Vol. 38, No. 3, 2003, pp. 174–76.

104 **This new mobilization centred around the cow:** Ibid.

105 **The announcement of elections in October 1989 had been preceded:** Asghar Ali Engineer, 'Communal Riots Before, During and After Lok Sabha Elections', *Economic and Political Weekly*, Vol. 26, No. 27, 1991, pp. 2135–138.

105 **were believed to have been complicit:** Engineer, 'Communal Frenzy', 1989.

106 **The cycles of flaring up of riots and their subsidence:** Paul R. Brass, *Theft of an Idol*; Steven I. Wilkinson, 'Communal Riots in India, *Economic and Political Weekly*, 2005, pp. 1–11; Wilkinson, *Votes and Violence: Electoral Competition and Ethnic Riots in India*, New York: Cambridge University Press, 2004.

106 **The invocation of emotionally charged notions of self:** Tej Parikh, 'Beef, Biryani and Indian Politics', *The Diplomat*, 16 September 2016; Nida Najar, 'Rumors of Cow Killing Deepen the Rift between Hindus and Muslims', *New York Times*, 14 October 2014.

113 **as they say, the 'victimized non-victims':** Nonica Datta, 'Memory and

History, A Daughter's Testimony', in Charu Gupta (ed.), *Gendering Colonial India: Reform, Print, Caste, and Communalism*, New Delhi: Orient Blackswan, 2012, pp. 287–316, p. 314; Violette G. J. Galonnier, 'Hindu-Muslim Communal Riots in India (1947-1886)', <https://www.sciencespo.fr/mass-violence-war-massacre-resistance/en/document/hindu-muslim-communal-riots-india-i-1947-1986> [accessed: 9 July 2019].

CHAPTER 8: A PARABLE OF OUR TIMES

115 **educated blacks were especially vulnerable:** Leon F. Litwack, 'The White Man's Fear of the Educated Negro: How the Negro Was Fitted for His Natural and Logical Calling', in the *Journal of Blacks in Higher Education*, No. 20, Summer 1998, pp. 100–08.

116 **When allowed to speak before being lynched:** James Allen, Hilton Als, John Lewis, Leon F. Litwack (eds.), *Without Sanctuary: Lynching Photography in America*, Sante Fe: Twin Palms Publisher, 2009, pp. 13, 14, and 17.

117 **It thrived on the myth of the 'black male rapist':** Robyn Wiegman, 'The Anatomy of Lynching', *Journal of the History of Sexuality*, Vol. 3, No. 3, Special Issue: African American Culture and Sexuality, January 1993, pp. 445–67.

117 **Each lynched black man was called 'big burly black brute':** Thomas Laquer, 'Lynched for Drinking From a White Men's Well', *London Review of Books*, Vol. 40, No. 19, 11 October 2018, pp. 11–15.

117 **The labour market's instability and a permissive government:** S. E. Tolnay and E. M. Beck, *A Festival of Violence: An Analysis of Southern Lynching*, 1882–1930, Urbana: University of Illinois Press, 1995.

118 **It was the firm conviction in one's own racial superiority:** Daniel J. Goldenhagen, *Hitler's Willing Executioners: Ordinary Germans and the Holocaust*, Vintage, 1997.

119 **'yellow fever and the malaria—the work of noxious insects':** As a Memphis merchant explained to an English visitor in 1909, in James Allen et al, *Without Sanctuary*.

119 **The photographs carried images of lynched bodies stripped:** The

image of the hanging bodies was immortalized in a song 'Strange Fruit' written by Abel Meeropol after he saw a lynching. The song was later sung by the famous jazz singer Billie Holiday. The strange fruit that the poplar trees in American South bore was 'black body swinging in the breeze' with 'blood on the leaves and blood at the root'.

119 The others gazed proudly at the camera: Ibid.

120 In this way lynching bound the white community: Amy Louise Wood, *Lynching and Spectacle: Witnessing Racial Violence in America, 1890-1940*, Chapel Hill: The University of North Carolina Press, 2009.

120 'One could not be a calm, cool, and detached scientist': W. E. B. Du Bois, *Dusk of Dawn*, New York: Schocken Books, 1940, 1968, p. 67.

120 Twain preferred to remain silent because he believed that he would: Mark Twain, 'The United States of Lyncherdom', available at <http://people.virginia.edu/~sfr/enam482e/lyncherdom.html> [accessed: 9 July 2019].

120 the majoritarian community deploys lynching: Anjan Ghosh, 'Upsurge in Mass Lynchings', *Economic and Political Weekly*, Vol. 20, No. 51/52, 21–28 December 1985, p. 2240; Gopal Guru, 'Understanding Violence against Dalits in Marathwada', *Economic and Political Weekly*, Vol. 29, No. 9, 26 February 1994, pp. 469–72; Nonica Datta, 'Politics of Cow Protection', *The Hindu*, 18 November 2002; Tanika Sarkar, 'Semiotics of Terror: Muslim Children and Women in Hindu Rashtra, *Economic and Political Weekly*, Vol. 37, No. 28, 2002, pp. 2872–76; Prakash Louis, 'Lynchings in Bihar: Reassertion of Dominant Castes', *Economic and Political Weekly*, Vol. 42, No. 44, 3–9 November 2007, pp. 26–28; Datta, 'Jharkhand Mob Lynchings Show Colonial Forms of Violence Flourish in Modern India', in the *Hindustan Times*, 27 June 2017; Sandipan Baksi and Aravindhan Nagarajan, 'Mob Lynchings in India: A Look at Data and the Story Behind the Numbers,' *Newslaundry*, 4 July 2017.

121 as a new phenomenon in Indian politics: Ziya Us Salam, *Lynch Files: The Forgotten Saga of Victims of Hate Crime*, New Delhi: Sage, 2019;

Apoorvanand, 'What is behind India's Epidemic of Mob Lynching?' *Al-Jazeera*, 6 July 2017; Prabhash K. Dutta, 'Story of Lynching', *India Today*, 25 June 2017.

121 'The volcano which was inactive for years has erupted': A VHP pamphlet titled 'Jihad', on <https://www.sabrang.com/cc/ archive/2002/marapril/pamphlet.htm> [accessed: 9 July 2019].

EPILOGUE

126 **Grain was bought from the nomadic Banjaras:** Ajay Dandekar, 'Landscapes in Conflict: Flocks, Hero-Stones, and Cult in Early Medieval Maharashtra', *Studies in History*, Vol. 7, No.2, 1991, pp. 301–24.

127 **The stories of pastoral communities have been absent:** Shereen Ratnagar, 'Pastoralism as an Issue in Historical Research', *Studies in History*, Vol. 7, No.2, 1991, pp. 181–93.

128 **To this day/ have you reared a pair of bullocks?:** Gogu Shyamala, 'Beef, Our Life', R. Srivatsan with help from Susie Tharu, N. Manohar and Jayasree Kalathil (trans.), available at <http://www.anveshi. org.in/beef-our-life-by-gogu-shyamala/> [accessed: 9 July 2019]. Reproduced by kind permission of the author.

131 **from 'states like Kerala, West Bengal, Arunachal Pradesh':** S. Anand, 'Thyagaraja's Cow', *Outlook*, 8 September 2003; Sahaya Noviston Lobo, 'The Mridangam Beat-Makers', *New Indian Express*, 8 October 2018; Ajayan, 'A Tiny Kerala Village Steeped in Drumbeats', *Livemint*, 29 December 2009; Ishita Bhatia, 'Howzat! Cow queers pitch for Cricket Balls', *Times of India*, 6 July 2016.

131 **Feasting on cattle was no longer a marker of ritual impurity:** Rowen Robinson, 'Negotiating Traditions: Popular Christianity in India', *Asian Journal of Social Science*, Vol. 37, No. 1, 2009, pp. 29–54; James Staples, '"Go On, Just Try Some!" Meat and Meaning-Making among South Indian Christians', *South Asia: Journal of South Asian Studies*, Vol. 31, No. 1, 2008, pp. 36–55.

131 **This is attested by Naga scholars:** J. H. Hutton, *The Angami Nagas*, Macmillan, 1921 and his *Sema Nagas*, Macmillan, 1921; J. P. Mills,

Lhota Nagas, Macmillan, 1922, *The Ao Nagas*, Macmillan, 1926, *Rengma Nagas*, Macmillan, 1937; Asoso Yonuo, *The Rising Nagas: A Historical and Political Study*, New Delhi: Manas Publications, 1948 (repr).

132 **Dalit autobiographies, poetry and songs talk about how their food was impacted:** Sharanya Deepak, 'There is no Dalit Cuisine: To Counter a History that is Far From Sweet', 20 November 2018 on popula.com; Rajyashri Goody, 'Eat with great Delight', 'Chavdar', 'What is the Caste of Water?', <www.rajyashrigoody.com> [accessed: 9 July 2019].

132 **The rarity of being able to fill your stomach:** Daya Pawar, *Baluta*, New Delhi: Speaking Tiger, 2015 (in Marathi in 1978).

132 **'Give us This Day a Feast of Flesh':** 'The Food on Our Plate', *Navayana* <https://navayana.org/blog/2014/12/18/the-food-on-our-plate/> [accessed: 9 July 2019]. Reproduced by kind permission of Navayana, New Delhi.

SELECT BIBLIOGRAPHY

Books

Adluri, Vishwa, and Joydeep Bagchee, *When the Goddess was a Woman: Mahabharata Ethnographies–Essays by Alf Hiltebeitel*, Vol. 2, Leiden: Brill, 2011.

Agrawal, Prem Narain, *Bhawani Dayal Sannyasi: A Public Worker of South Africa*, Uttar Pradesh: The Indian Colonial Association, 1939.

Allen, James, Hilton Als, John Lewis, Leon F. Litwack (eds.), *Without Sanctuary: Lynching Photography in America*, Sante Fe: Twin Palms Publisher, 2009.

Bagul, Baburao, *When I Hid my Caste: Stories*, New Delhi: Speaking Tiger, 2018.

Barz, Richard, *The Bhakti Sect of Vallabhacharya*, Delhi: Munshiram Manoharlal, 1992.

'Bedhadak' Subhash, *Sampurna Khatu Shyam Itihaas*, Jaipur: Roodmal Bookseller, undated.

Bennett, Peter, *The Path of Grace: Social Organisation and Temple Worship in a Vaishnava Sect*, Delhi: Hindustan Publishing Corporation, 1993.

Bhardwaj, Suraj Bhan, *Contestations and Accommodations: Mewat and Meos in Mughal India*, New Delhi: Oxford University Press, 2016.

Bharucha, Rustom, *Rajasthan: An Oral History—Conversations with Komal Kothari*, New Delhi: Penguin Books, 2015.

Brass, Paul R., *Theft of an Idol: Text and Context in the Representation of Collective Violence*, Princeton: Princeton University Press, 1997.

Busch, Allison, *Poetry of Kings: The Classical Hindi Literature of Mughal India*, New York: Oxford University Press, 2011.

Canetti, Elias, *Crowds and Power*, New York: Continuum, 1960, 1973 (repr).

Chakrabarti, Kunal, *Religious Process: The Puranas and the Making of a Religious Tradition*, New Delhi: Oxford University Press, 2001.

Chatterjee, Partha, and Anjan Ghosh (eds.), *History and The Present*, New Delhi: Permanent Black, 2002.

Dangle, Arjun (ed.), *Poisoned Bread*, New Delhi: Orient Blackswan, 2009, 2018.

Darnton, Robert, *The Forbidden Best-sellers of Pre-Revolutionary France*, London: Fontana, 1996.

Datta, Nonica, *Forming an Identity: A Social History of the Jats*, New Delhi: Oxford University Press, 1999.

Deshpande, G. P., *Selected Writings of Jotirao Phule*, New Delhi: Leftword Books, 2002.

Dhali, Rajshree, 'Popular Religion in Rajasthan: A Study of Four Deities and their Worship in Nineteenth and Twentieth Century', PhD Thesis, Jawaharlal Nehru University, 2004 <http://shodhganga.inflibnet.ac.in/handle/10603/15372> [accessed: 9 July 2019].

Du Bois, W. E. B., *Dusk of Dawn*, New York: Schocken Books, 1940, 1968 (repr).

Eaton, Richard, *The Rise of Islam and the Bengal Frontier, 1204–1760*, Berkeley: University of California Press, 1993.

Figueira, Dorothy M., *Aryans, Jews, Brahmins Theorizing Authority Through Myths of Identity*, New Delhi: Navayana, 2002, 2015 (repr).

Goldenhagen, Daniel J., *Hitler's Willing Executioners: Ordinary Germans and the Holocaust*, New York: Knopf, 1996.

Gupta, Anand Swarup, *The Vamana Purana*, Varanasi: All India Kashiraj Trust, 1967.

Hardyalsingh, Raibahadur Munshi, *Report Mardumshumari Rajmarwaad, 1891: Rajasthan ki Jatiyon ka Itihas man Ritiriwaaz*, Jodhpur: Maharaj Mansingh Pustak Prakash Shodh Kendra, 1894, 2010 (repr).

Hauser, Walter and Kailash Chandra Jha, *My Life's Struggle: A Translation of Swami Sahajanand Sarawati's Mera Jivan Sangharsh*, New Delhi: Manohar, 2016.

Hauser, Walter, *The Bihar Provincial Kisan Sabha 1929-1942: A Study of an Indian Peasant Movement*, New Delhi, Manohar, 2019.

Jaffrelot, Christophe, *Dr. Ambedkar and Untouchability: Analysing and Fighting Caste*, London: Hurst, 2000, 2005 (repr).

Kumar, Mayank, *Monsoon Ecologies: Irrigation, Agriculture and Settlement Patterns in Rajasthan During the Pre-Colonial Period*, New Delhi: Manohar, 2013.

Lyons, Tryna, *The Artists of Nathdwara: the Practice of Painting in Rajasthan*, Bloomington: Indian University Press, 2004.

Menon, Kalyani Devaki, *Everyday Nationalism: Women of the Hindu Right in India*, Philadelphia: University of Pennsylvania Press, 2012.

Oak, P. N., *The Taj Mahal is a Hindu Palace*, Bombay: Pearl Books, 1968.

Oberoi, Harjot, *The Construction of Religious Boundaries: Culture, Identity and Diversity in Sikh Tradition*, Chicago: University of Chicago Press, 1994.

Omvedt, Gail, *Seeking Begumpura: The Social Vision of Anticaste Intellectuals*, New Delhi: Navayana, 2008, 2016 (repr).

Pandey, Gyanendra, *The Construction of Communalism in Colonial North India*, New Delhi: Oxford University Press, 1990, 2006 (repr).

Pandian, M. S. S., *Brahmin and Non-Brahmin: Genealogies of the Tamil Political Present*, Ranikhet: Permanent Black, 2007, 2016 (repr).

Pargiter, F. E., *Ancient Indian Historical Tradition*, London: Oxford University Press, 1922.

Parshad, Vijay, *Untouchable Freedom: A Social History of Dalit Community*, New Delhi: Oxford University Press, 2000.

Pattanaik, Devdutt, *Jaya: An Illustrated Retelling of Mahabharata*, New Delhi: Penguin Books, 2010.

_____, *Shyam*, New Delhi: Penguin Books, 2018.

Pawar, Daya, *Baluta*, Jerry Pinto (trans.), New Delhi: Speaking Tiger, 2015.

Pemaram, *Madhyakaleen Rajasthan mein Dharmik Andolan*, Ajmer: Archana Prakashan, 1977.

Prasad, Durga, *English Translation of Satyarth Prakash*, Lahore: Virajnand Press, 1908.

Saha, Shandip, Creating a Community of Grace: A History of the *Pushti Marga* in Northern and Western India (1479–1905), PhD thesis submitted to University of Ottawa, 2004.

Sarkar, Sumit, *Modern India: 1885-1947*, Gurgaon: Macmillan, 1983, 2013 (repr).

Seal, Anil, *The Emergence of Indian Nationalism: Competition and Collaboration in the Later Nineteenth Century*, Cambridge: Cambridge University Press, 1968.

Singh, Upinder, *Political Violence in Ancient India*, Cambridge: Harvard University Press, 2017.

Skanda Purana, Maheshwarkhand-Kumarikakhand, Gorakhpur: Gita Press, undated.

Sleeman, W. H., *Rambles and Recollections of an Indian Official*, New Delhi: Oxford University Press, 1893, 1915.

Soifer, Deborah, *The Myths of Narasimha and Vamana: Two Avatars in Cosmological Perspective*, Albany: State University of New York Press, 1991.

Sreenivasan, Ramya, *Many Lives of Rajput Queen: Heroic Pasts in India, c.1500–1900*, Seattle: University of Washington Press, 2007.

Stewart, Tony K., *The Final Word: The Caitanya Caritamrta and the Grammar of Religious Tradition*, New York: Oxford University Press, 2010.

Swami Dayanand Saraswati, *Gaukarunanidhi*, Delhi: Arsh Sahitya Prachar Trust, 1881, 1998 (repr).

_____, *Satyarth Prakash*, Delhi: Arsh Sahitya Prakash Trust, 2008, 1875.

Swami Vaidikanand, *Swami Dayanand ke Amrit Vachan*, Bhaag 2, 4th edition, Indore: Swami Dayanand Brhamgyan Ashram Nyas, 2007.

Thapar, Romila, *Sakuntala: Texts, Readings, Histories*, New York: Columbia University Press, 2011.

Thursby, G. R., *Hindu-Muslim Relations in British India: A Study of Controversy, Conflict, and Communal Movements in Northern India, 1923–1928*, Leiden: Brill, 1975.

Tolnay, S. E. and E. M. Beck, *A Festival of Violence: An Analysis of Southern Lynching, 1882–1930*, Urbana: University of Illinois Press, 1995.

Van der Veer, Peter, *Religious Nationalism: Hindus and Muslims in India*, New Delhi: Oxford University Press, 1994.

Veyne, Paul, *Did the Greeks Believe in Their Myths? An Essay on the*

Constitutive Imagination, Chicago: University of Chicago Press, 1988.

Vimalkirti, L. J. Meshram, *Jotiba Phule Rachnavali* (Hindi Translation), Delhi: Prakashan, undated.

Wilkinson, Steven I., *Votes and Violence: Electoral Competition and Ethnic Riots in India*, New York: Cambridge University Press, 2004.

Wood, Amy Louise, *Lynching and Spectacle: Witnessing Racial Violence in America, 1890-1940*, Chapel Hill: The University of North Carolina Press, 2009.

Articles and Book Chapters

Bellwinkel-Schempp, Maren, 'Kabir-Panthis in Kanpur: From Sampradaya to Dalit Identity', in Monika Horstmann (ed.), *Images of Kabir*, New Delhi: Manohar, 2002.

_____, 'Pigs and Power: Urban Space and Urban Decay', in Evelin Hust and Michael Mann (eds.), *Urbanization and Governance in India*, Manohar, New Delhi, 2005.

_____, 'The Khatiks of Kanpur and the Bristle Trade: Towards an Anthropology of man and beast', *Sociological Bulletin*, Vol. 47, No. 2 1998.

Bharucha, Rustom, 'Muslims and Others: Anecdotes, Fragments and Uncertainties of Evidence', *Economic and Political Weekly*, Vol. 38, No. 40, 2003.

Bhattacharya, Neeladri, 'Predicaments of Secular Histories', *Public Culture*, Vol. 20, No. 1, 2008.

Brosius, Christiane, 'Hindutva Intervisuality: Videos and the Politics of Representation', *Contributions to Indian Sociology*, Vol. 36, No. 1 & 2, 2002.

Burchett, Patton, 'Bhakti Rhetoric in the Hagiography of 'Untouchable' Saints: Discerning Bhakti's Ambivalence on Caste and Brahminhood', *International Journal of Hindu Studies*, Vol. 13, No. 2, August 2009.

Chattopadhyaya, B. D., 'Origin of the Rajputs: The Political, Economic and Social Processes in Early Medieval Rajasthan', *The Making of Early Medieval India*, New Delhi: Oxford University Press, 1994, 2001 (repr).

Chattopadhyaya, Brajadulal, 'Representing the Other? Sanskrit Sources and the Muslims (Eight to Fourteenth Century)', in Aloka Parasher-

Sen (ed.), *Subordinate and Marginal Groups in Early India*, New Delhi: Oxford University Press, 2004.

Chigateri, Shraddha, 'Negotiating the 'Sacred' Cow: Cow Slaughter and the Regulation of Difference in India', in M. Mookherjee (ed.), *Democracy, Religious Pluralism and the Liberal Dilemma of Accommodation*, Studies in Global Justice, Vol. 7, Dodrecht: Springer, 2011.

Cohen, Percy S., 'Theories of Myth,' *Man*, New Series, Vol. 4, No. 3, September 1969.

Copland, Ian, 'What to Do about Cows? Princely versus British Approaches to a South Asian Dilemma', *Bulletin of the School of Oriental and African Studies*, London: University of London, Vol. 68, No. 1, 2005.

Crooke, William, 'The Veneration of the Cow in India,' *Folklore*, 1912.

Dandekar, Ajay, 'Landscapes in Conflict: Flocks, Hero-Stones, and Cult in Early Medieval Maharashtra', *Studies in History*, Vol. 7, No. 2, 1991.

Darnton, Robert, 'Peasant Tell Tales: The meaning of Mother Goose', *The Great Cat Massacre: and other Episodes in French Cultural History*, Basic Books, 1999, 2009 (repr).

Datta, Nonica, 'Hinduisation of the Balmikis', *Economic and Political Weekly*, Vol. 35, No. 41, 7–13 October, 2000.

Datta, Nonica, 'Memory and History, A Daughter's Testimony', Charu Gupta (ed.), *Gendering Colonial India: Reform, Print, Caste, and Communalism*, New Delhi: Orient Blackswan, 2012.

Davis, Richard H., 'The Iconography of Rama's Chariot', David Ludden (ed.), *Making India Hindu: Religion, Community, and the Politics of Democracy in India*, New Delhi: Oxford University Press, 1996.

Desai, Santosh, 'Ramayana–An Instrument of Historical Contact and Cultural Transmission between India and Asia', *The Journal of Asian Studies*, Vol. 30, No. 1, November 1970.

Dhali, Rajshree, 'Pilgrimage to the Abode of a Folk Deity', *International Journal of Religious Tourism and Pilgrimage*, Vol. 4, No. 6, 2016.

Eaton, in Richard, 'Approaches to Study of Conversion to Islam in India', Richard C. Martin (ed.), *Approaches to Islam in Religious Studies*, Tucson: University of Arizona Press, 1985.

_____, 'Chapter 5: Mass Conversion to Islam: Theories and

Protagonists', *The Rise of Islam and the Bengal Frontier, 1204-1760*, Berkeley: University of California Press, 1993.

_____, 'The Political and Religious Authority of the Shrine of Baba Farid', in his *Essays on Islam in Indian History*, New Delhi: Oxford University Press, 2000.

Engineer, Asghar Ali, 'Communal Frenzy at Indore', *Economic and Political Weekly*, Vol. 24, No. 44/45, 4-11 November 1989.

_____, 'Communal Riots Before, During and After Lok Sabha Elections', *Economic and Political Weekly*, Vol. 26, No. 37, 1991.

Farmer, Victoria L., 'Mass Media: Images, Mobilization, and Communalism', in David Ludden (ed.), *Making India Hindu: Religion, Community, and the Politics of Democracy in India*, New Delhi: Oxford University Press, 1996.

Freitag, Sandra, 'Contesting in Public: Colonial Legacies and Contemporary Communalism', in Ludden, *Making India Hindu*.

Freitag, Sandra, '"Natural Leaders", Administrators and Social Control: Communal Riots in the United Provinces, 1870-1925', *South Asia: Journal of South Asian Studies*, Vol. 1, No. 2, 1978.

_____, 'Sacred Symbol as Mobilizing Ideology: The North Indian Search for a "Hindu" Community', *Comparative Studies in Society and History*, Vol. 22, No. 4, October 1980.

Gadgil, Madhav and Kailash Malhotra, 'Ecology of a Pastoral Caste: Gavli Dhangars of Peninsular India', *Human Ecology*, Vol. 10, No. 1, 1982.

Gaston, Anne-Marie, 'Continuity of Tradition in the Music of Nathdvara: A Participant-Observer's View', Karine Schomer et al (eds.), *The Idea of Rajasthan: Explorations in Regional Identity*, Vol. 1, Delhi: Manohar, 2001.

Ghosh, Anjan, 'Upsurge in Mass Lynchings', *Economic and Political Weekly*, Vol. 20, No. 51/52, 21–28 December 1985.

Gokhale-Turner, Jayashree B., 'Bhakti or Vidroha: Continuity and Change in Dalit Sahitya', in Jayant Lele (ed.), *Tradition and Modernity in Bhakti Movements*, Leiden: Brill, 1981.

Guha, Sumit, 'Forest Polities and Agrarian Empires: The Khandesh Bhils, c.1700-1850, *Indian Economic and Social History Review*, Vol. 33, No. 2, 1996.

Gupta, Charu, 'Articulating Hindu Masculinity and Femininity: "Shuddhi" and "Sangathan" Movements in United Provinces in the 1920s, *Economic and Political Weekly*, Vol. 33, No. 13, 26 March–3 April 1998.

_____, 'Feminine, Criminal or Manly: Imaging Dalit Masculinities in Colonial North India', *Indian Economic and Social History Review*, Vol. 47, No. 3, 2010.

_____, 'Intimate Desires: Dalit Women and Religious Conversion in Colonial India, *The Journal of Asian Studies*, Vol. 73, No. 3, 2014.

_____, 'The Icon of Mother in Late Colonial North India: "Bharat Mata", "Matro Bhasha" and "Gau Mata"', *Economic and Political Weekly*, Vol. 36, No. 45, 2001.

Guru, Gopal, 'Understanding Violence against Dalits in Marathwada', *Economic and Political Weekly*, Vol. 29, No. 9, 26 February 1994.

Hardiman, David, 'Power in the Forest: The Dangs 1820-1940', David Arnold and David Hardiman (eds.), *Subaltern Studies VIII*, Delhi: Oxford University Press, 1994.

Jodhka, Surinder and Murli Dhar, 'Cow, Caste and Communal Politics Dalit Killings in Jhajjar', *Economic and Political Weekly*, Vol. 38, No. 3, 2003.

Litwack, Leon F., 'The White Man's Fear of the Educated Negro: How the Negro Was Fitted for His Natural and Logical Calling', *The Journal of Blacks in Higher Education*, No. 20, Summer 1998.

Louis, Prakash, 'Lynchings in Bihar: Reassertion of Dominant Castes', *Economic and Political Weekly*, Vol. 42, No. 44, 3–9 November 2007.

Mittal, S. K., and Kapil Kumar, 'Baba Ram Chandra and Peasant Upsurge in Oudh: 1920-21', *Social Scientist*, Vol. 6, No. 11, 1978.

Murthy, M. L. K., and Günther D. Sontheimer, 'Prehistoric Background to Pastoralism in the Southern Deccan in the Light of Oral Traditions and Cults of some Pastoral Communities', *Anthropos*, 1980.

Nandy, Ashis, 'History's Forgotten Doubles', *History and Theory*, Vol. 34, No. 2, 1995.

O'Toole, Theresa, 'Secularizing the Sacred Cow: The Relationship between Religious Reform and Hindu Nationalism', in Antony Copley (ed.), *Hinduism in Public and Private: Reform, Hindutva, Gender and Sampraday*, New Delhi: Oxford University Press, 2003.

Omvedt, Gail, 'Jotirao Phule and the Ideology of Social Revolution in India,' *Economic and Political Weekly*, Vol. 6, No. 37, 11 September 1971.

_____, 'Review: Shivaji and Maratha "Swarajya"', *Economic and Political Weekly*, Vol. 24, No. 1, 7 January 1989.

_____, 'The Satyashodhak Samaj and Peasant Agitation', *Economic and Political Weekly*, Vol. 8, No. 44, 3 November 1973.

Parasher-Sen, Aloka, '"Foreigner" and "Tribe" as Barbarian (*Mleccha*) in Early North India', *Subordinate and Marginal Groups in Early India*, New Delhi: Oxford University Press, 2004.

Patankar, Bharat and Gail Omvedt, 'The Dalit Liberation Movement in Colonial Period', *Economic and Political Weekly*, Vol. 14, No. 7/8, Annual Number: Class and Caste in India, February 1979.

Pawar, Daya, 'Oh! Great Poet', Graham Smith (trans.), in Sanjay Paswan and Pramanshi Jaideva (eds.), *Encyclopaedia of Dalits in India*, Vol. 11, Delhi: Kalpaz Publications, 2002.

_____, *Baluta*, New Delhi: Speaking Tiger, 2015 (in Marathi in 1978).

Peabody, Norbert, 'Disciplining the Body, Disciplining the Body-Politic: Physical Culture and Social Violence among North Indian Wrestlers', *Comparative Studies in Society and History*, Vol. 51, No. 2, April 2009.

_____, 'In Whose Turban Does the Lord Reside?: The Objectification of Charisma and the Fetishism of Objects in the Hindu Kingdom of Kota, *Comparative Studies in Society and History*, Vol. 33, No. 4, 1991.

Pinch, William R., 'Soldier Monks and Militant Sadhus', in Ludden (ed.), *Making India Hindu*.

Pinney, Christopher, 'The Nation (Un)Pictured? Chromolithography and "Popular" Politics in India', 1878–1995, *Critical Inquiry*, Vol. 23, No. 4, Summer 1997.

Ramanujan, A. K., 'Three Hundred Ramayanas: Five Examples and Three Thoughts on Translation,' in Vinay Dharwadker (ed.), *The Collected Essays of A. K. Ramanujan*, New Delhi: Oxford University Press, 1999.

Ratnagar, Shereen, 'Pastoralism as an Issue in Historical Research', *Studies in History*, Vol. 7, No. 2, 1991.

Robb, Peter, 'The Challenge of Gau Mata: British Policy and Religious Change in India, 1880–1916', *Modern Asian Studies*, Vol. 20, No. 2, 1986.

Robinson, Rowen, 'Negotiating Traditions: Popular Christianity in India', *Asian Journal of Social Science*, Vol. 37, No. 1, 2009.

Saha, Shandip, 'The Movement of Bhakti along a North-West Axis: Tracing the History of the Pushti Marg between the Sixteenth and Nineteenth Centuries', *International Journal of Hindu Studies*, Vol. 11, No. 3, December 2007.

Salam, Ziya us, *Lynch Files: The Forgotten Saga of Victims of Hate Crime*, New Delhi: SAGE, 2019.

Sarkar, Tanika, 'Semiotics of Terror: Muslim Children and Women in Hindu Rashtra, *Economic and Political Weekly*, Vol. 37, No. 28, 2002.

Siddiqi, Asiya, 'Ayesha's World: A Butcher's Family in Nineteenth-Century Bombay', *Comparative Studies in Society and History*, Vol. 43, No. 1, June 2001.

Singh, Lata, 'The Bihar Kisan Sabha Movement-1933-1939', *Social Scientist*, Vol. 20, No. 5/6, 1992.

Smith, Brian K. and Wendy Doniger, 'Sacrifice and Substitution: Ritual Mystification and Mythical Demystification', Numen, Vol. 36, Fasc. 2, December, 1989.

Sreenivasan, Ramya, 'Rethinking Kingship and Authority in South Asia: Amber (Rajasthan), ca, 1560–1615, *Journal of the Economic and Social History of the Orient*, Vol. 57, No. 4, 2014.

Staples, James, 'Go On, Just Try Some!' Meat and Meaning-Making among South Indian Christians', *South Asia: Journal of South Asian Studies*, Vol. 31, No.1, 2008.

Talbot, Cynthia, 'Becoming Turk the Rajput Way: Conversion and Identity in an Indian Warrior Narrative', *Modern Asian Studies*, Vol. 43, No. 1, 2009.

Tambiah, Stanley J., 'Some Reflections on Communal Violence in South Asia', *Journal of Asian Studies*, Vol. 49, No. 4, 1990 and *Leveling Crowds: Ethnonationalist Conflicts and Collective Violence in South Asia*, Berkeley: University of California Press, 1996.

Thapar, Romila, 'The Theory of Aryan Race and India: History and Politics', *Cultural Pasts: Essays in Early Indian History*, New Delhi: Oxford University Press, 2000.

Trautmann, Thomas R., 'Introduction', *The Aryan Debate*, New Delhi: Oxford University Press, 2005.

Wiegman, Robyn, 'The Anatomy of Lynching', *Journal of the History of Sexuality*, Vol. 3, No. 3, Special Issue: African American Culture and Sexuality, January 1993.

Wilkinson, Steven, 'Communal Riots in India', *Economic and Political Weekly*, 2005.

Yang, Anand A., 'Sacred Symbol and Sacred Space in Rural India: Community Mobilization in the "Anti-Cow Killing" Riot of 1893', *Comparative Studies in Society and History*, Vol. 22, No. 4, 1980.

Newspaper and Online Articles

'The States where Cow Slaughter is Legal in India', *Indian Express,* 8 October 2015.

Ajayan, 'A Tiny Kerala Village Steeped in Drumbeats', *Live Mint*, 29 December 2009; Ishita Bhatia, 'Howzat! Cow queers pitch for Cricket Balls', *Times of India*, 6 July 2016.

Anand, S., 'Thyagaraja's Cow', *Outlook*, 8 September 2003.

Apoorvanand, 'What is behind India's Epidemic of Mob Lynching?' *Al-Jazeera*, 6 July 2017.

Baksi, Sandipan and Aravindhan Nagarajan, 'Mob Lynchings in India: A Look at Data and the Story Behind the Numbers', *Newslaundry*, 4 July 2017.

Datta, Nonica 'Politics of Cow Protection', *The Hindu*, 18 November 2002.

_____, 'Jharkhand Mob Lynchings Show Colonial Forms of Violence Flourish in Modern India', *Hindustan Times*, 27 June 2017.

Deepak, Sharanya, 'There is no Dalit Cuisine: To Counter A History that is Far From Sweet', *Popula*, 20 November 2018, available at < https://popula.com/2018/11/20/there-is-no-dalit-cuisine/> [accessed: 10 September 2019].

Dutta, Prabash K., 'Is Ban on Sale of Cattle for Slaughter Unconstitutional: A Fact Check', *India Today*, 16 June 2017.

_____, 'Story of Lynching', *India Today*, 25 June 2017.

Galonnier, Violet G. J., 'Hindu Muslim Communal Riots in India, II

(1986–2011), 2013, <http://www.sciencespo.fr/mass-violence-war-massacre-resistance/en/document/hindu-muslim-communal-riots-india-ii-1986-2011> [accessed: 9 July 2019].

Galonnier, Violette G. J., 'Hindu-Muslim Communal Riots in India (1947–1886)', <https://www.sciencespo.fr/mass-violence-war-massacre-resistance/en/document/hindu-muslim-communal-riots-india-i-1947-1986> [accessed: 9 July 2019].

Goody, Rajyashri, 'Eat with great Delight', 'Chavdar', 'What is the Caste of Water?' available at <http://www.rajyashrigoody.com> [accessed: 9 July 2019].

Laquer, Thomas, 'Lynched for Drinking From a White Men's Well', *London Review of Books*, Vol. 40, No. 19, 11 October 2018, pp. 11–15.

Lobo, Sahaya Noviston, 'The Mridangam Beat-Makers', *New Indian Express*, 8 October 2018.

Najar, Nida, 'Rumors of Cow Killing Deepen the Rift between Hindus and Muslims', *New York Times*, 14 October 2014.

Narke, Hari, 'Dnyanajyoti Savitribai Phule I and II', 6 September and 1 October 2012, *Round Table India*, available at <https://www.roundtableindia.org/> [accessed: 10 September 2019].

Parikh, Tej, 'Beef, Biryani and Indian Politics', *The Diplomat*, 16 September 2016.

Shyamala, Gogu, 'Beef, Our Life', Translated by R. Srivatsan with help from Susie Tharu, N. Manohar and Jayasree Kalathil, available at <http://www.anveshi.org.in/beef-our-life-by-gogu-shyamala/> [accessed: 10 September 2019].

Singh, Tavleen, 'Shah Bano Makes a Dramatic Turnaround', *India Today*, 15 December 1985.

Sinha, Bhadra, 'Cattle Trade for Slaughter: Supreme Court Suspends ban Across India', *Hindustan Times*, 12 July 2017.

Sinha, Surajit, 'State Formation and the Rajput Myth in Central India', *Man in India*, Vol. 42, No. 1, 1964.

Ziegler, Norman P., 'Evolution of the Rathore State of Marvar: Structural Change and Warfare', in Karine Schomer et al (eds.), *The Idea of Rajasthan: Explorations in Regional Identity*, Vol. 2, Delhi: Manohar, 2001.

Websites
Anveshi
Round Table India
Rajyashri Goody
Sciences Po